W9-AEB-331

The Dragon Network

Since 1996, Bloomberg Press has published books for financial professionals, as well as books of general interest in investing, economics, current affairs, and policy affecting investors and business people. Titles are written by well-known practitioners, BLOOMBERG NEWS® reporters and columnists, and other leading authorities and journalists. Bloomberg Press books have been translated into more than 20 languages.

For a list of available titles, please visit our web site at www.wiley.com/go/bloombergpress.

The Dragon Network

Inside Stories of the Most Successful Chinese Family Businesses

A.B. Susanto
Patricia Susanto

Published by John Wiley & Sons Singapore Pte. Ltd.
1 Fusionopolis Walk, #07-01, Solaris South Tower, Singapore 138628

Other Wiley Editorial Offices
John Wiley & Sons, 111 River Street, Hoboken, NJ 07030, USA
John Wiley & Sons, The Atrium, Southern Gate, Chichester, West Sussex, P019 8SQ, United Kingdom
John Wiley & Sons (Canada) Ltd., 5353 Dundas Street West, Suite 400, Toronto, Ontario, M9B 6HB, Canada
John Wiley & Sons Australia Ltd., 42 McDougall Street, Milton, Queensland 4064, Australia
Wiley-VCH, Boschstrasse 12, D-69469 Weinheim, Germany

ISBN 978-1-118-33937-4 (Cloth)
ISBN 978-1-118-33938-1 (ePDF)
ISBN 978-1-118-33939-8 (Mobi)
ISBN 978-1-118-33940-4 (ePub)

Typeset in 11.5/14 pt. Bembo Std. by MPS Limited, Chennai, India.
Printed in Singapore by Ho Printing Pte. Ltd.

10 9 8 7 6 5 4 3 2 1

Contents

Acknowledgments

I would like to express our gratitude to all of our family who have taken the time to meet with us and share their story and impart their wisdom and knowledge of life; the experience itself is nothing short of extraordinary. We have also appreciated the support from the Indonesia Chinese community, who have given their time to be interviewed, helping us go deeper into the roots of our Chinese heritage.

Thanks go to our team, especially Himawan Wijanarko and Hariadi Suripto, who have dedicated their time to conducting extensive research, holding discussions, and writing this book, and to the team at John Wiley & Sons, who have made an idea come true.

Introduction

Overseas Chinese family businesses (OCFBs) have played an important role in the Southeast Asian economies of Indonesia, Thailand, Malaysia, Singapore, and the Philippines. In other parts of the world, such as Australia and North America, we can also find successful family businesses founded by Chinese citizens, although their number and size are smaller than those in the Southeast Asia region.

As most Chinese family businesses come from the Southeast Asia region it is important to know some of the reasons. First, countries such as Indonesia, Thailand, Malaysia, and the Philippines are emerging markets—nations with social or business activity in the process of rapid growth and industrialization. The role of these emerging markets, together with other quickly growing markets from other countries such as Brazil, India, and China, are expected to be increasingly important in the upcoming decades. To support this rapid growth and industrialization, the contribution of these Chinese-owned businesses cannot be ignored.

Second, all countries in the Southeast Asia region are members of the Association of Southeast Asian Nations (ASEAN). ASEAN covers a land area of 4.46 million km^2, which is 3 percent of the total land area of Earth, and has a population of approximately 600 million people, which is 8.8 percent of the world's population. In 2010, its combined nominal GDP had grown to US$1.8 trillion. If ASEAN were a single entity, it would rank as the ninth largest economy in the world, behind the United States, China, Japan, Germany, France, Brazil, the United Kingdom, and Italy. ASEAN will make much progress in economic integration by creating an ASEAN Economic Community (AEC) by 2015. Overseas Chinese family businesses, already known for their ability to identify and capitalize on business opportunities, surely do not want to miss the chance to tap into this large and potential market.

Third is the signing of the ASEAN−China Free Trade Area (ACFTA). ACFTA is a free-trade area among the ten member nations of the ASEAN plus China. This free-trade area came into effect on January 1, 2010. ACFTA is the largest free-trade area in terms of population and third largest in terms of nominal GDP. It also has the third largest trade volume after the European Economic Area and the North American Free Trade Area (NAFTA). China had already overtaken the United States as the third largest trading partner of ASEAN, after Japan and the European Union, when the free-trade area came into effect. China is also the world's largest exporter, so Chinese-owned businesses can be expected to seek opportunities to increase their business value.

The rapid growth and development of the Chinese economy has drawn attention from people around the world. They want to learn about the characteristics of the Chinese economy, including how Chinese businesspeople run their companies. Since the economic reform and the integration into world society of China, the number of non-state businesses has increased and many of them are family owned. Today, Chinese family companies control a portion of Asia's economic wealth that is larger than their relative share in population (Lee, 2006). This development will attract more people to research Chinese family businesses. And to make the learning process easier, people outside mainland China will likely observe family businesses founded by ethnic Chinese in their home countries, since these businesses are considered to have many similarities with family businesses in mainland China.

Economic development in the ASEAN and mainland China, as well as success stories of ethnic Chinese entrepreneurs in other regions such as North America and Australia, are the reason why learning about OCFBs is needed. Most ethnic Chinese businesses are family owned since family is the foundation of Chinese organizations, including businesses. We need to learn their management style, for example, how business organization is structured, how family relationship affects business management, and how Chinese traditional values influence family business practices. It is also interesting to learn about the challenges facing Chinese family businesses in a rapidly changing environment, and whether these family businesses will be able to survive and thrive in future generations.

Chapter 1

Revealing Fast-Growing Overseas Chinese Family Businesses

In every country or region, there are always people who move and live outside their area for many reasons. Chinese people are no exception. Many of them have left and then lived outside of China. These people are known as *overseas Chinese*. The word "China" as denoted here includes the People's Republic of China (also known as mainland China), Taiwan, Hong Kong, and Macau. Hong Kong and Macau are part of the People's Republic of China, while the status of Taiwan as a state is still disputed.

Many Chinese people migrated to various regions in Southeast Asia, North America, Australia, Europe, Latin America, and Africa. These people then created a community in every place in which they settled. Many Chinese people left their home country due to political instability, wars, starvation, poverty, and rampant corruption. Most of them were poor, were poorly educated, and were illiterate. Many of them worked as a laborer for low wages.

Between 1840 and 1940, about 20 to 22 million Chinese people left their country to live in other regions, according to McKeown (2010). Southeast Asian countries such as Malaysia, Singapore, Indonesia, Thailand, Vietnam, and the Philippines became their main destinations. Most of these people found work in mines and on plantations. About 75 percent of them then went back to China once their contracts had expired, while the rest stayed and started to build small family businesses. These businesses served as the middlemen in export and import activities, connecting local markets, as well as Southeast Asians.

Currently, there are about 50 million overseas Chinese people around the world. Most of them live in Southeast Asia, and location proximity might be the reason why most of these Chinese people chose to move to this region. Singapore is the only country in the world outside of China where ethnic Chinese constitute the majority of its people. In countries such as Malaysia, Indonesia, Thailand, the Philippines, and Vietnam, overseas Chinese make up a large minority. Many overseas Chinese come from regions such as Guangdong, Fujian, and Hainan, and most work in the area of commerce and finance, where their contribution to the economic development in this area is very significant. This is different with overseas Chinese living in North America, Europe, and Australia, where their professions are varied, such as lecturers, doctors, and artists.

Migration by Chinese people to western countries—such as the United States, Canada, Australia, New Zealand, and Europe, as well as to Latin American countries such as Mexico, Peru, and Panama—began in the 19th century. Nevertheless, their number was much smaller compared to those moving to Southeast Asia. In 2010, for example, in Germany the number of ethnic Chinese was about 76,000 people. In Austria, the number was about 15,000 to 30,000 people.

The number of overseas Chinese in South Korea was less than 30,000 people, according to Hyung-Jin (2006). Recently, the Chinese government has made an effort to strengthen their relationships with African countries, along with the continent's higher economic growth. Many Chinese companies are involved in infrastructure development, and Chinese people can be found in African countries such as South Africa, Nigeria, Namibia, Zambia, Algeria, and Angola. In Russia, the number of ethnic Chinese in the Far East region has increased significantly. In 2006, the number was almost 1 million, while in 1989 the number was 2,000. In the next two to three decades, Chinese are expected to become a dominant ethnic group in the Far East region.

Overseas Chinese often transfer money back home to improve the living conditions of their family and relatives. Overseas Chinese also play an important role in the rising economy of China. Many of them have set up businesses in the country, which has now overtaken Japan as the second largest economy in the world.

For Chinese, ethnic background is usually more important than nationality or citizenship. Someone is considered Chinese if he or she is of Chinese descent, regardless of where they live. And he or she will be classified as overseas Chinese if they live outside China.

Assimilation

Assimilation refers to a situation where newcomers that have different cultures arrive in a new place. In the next stage, both newcomers and the host society contribute some of their cultures and create a new society with a new culture. Communication plays an important role in shaping the new culture. This process takes place gradually, and the degree of assimilation varies. Full assimilation occurs when the differences between newcomers and the host society no longer exist.

Overseas Chinese vary widely regarding their degree of assimilation with the host society. The most successful assimilation happens in Thailand. King Rama I, the founder of the Chakri Dynasty and the current monarch, is half Chinese. His predecessor, King Taksin, is the son of an ethnic Chinese from Guangdong province who migrated to Thailand. King Taksin's mother, Nok-iang, is a Thai. In Burma, overseas Chinese adopt Burmese culture while at the same time maintaining their culture and tradition.

In Indonesia, Singapore, Brunei, and Malaysia, overseas Chinese have a strong and visible cultural identity, and the same thing often happens in western countries. In the Philippines, there is a difference in the degree of assimilation between the younger and older generations of overseas Chinese. While younger generations can assimilate well, the older ones still consider themselves outsiders.

Discrimination

Discrimination is the prejudicial treatment of individuals based on their membership, or perceived membership, in a certain group, such as race, ethnicity, religion, skin color, etc. It involves the group's initial reaction or interaction, influencing someone's behavior toward the group, restricting members of one group from opportunities that are available to another group, leading to the exclusion of the individual or group based on logical or irrational decision making.

Most of the early generations of Chinese immigrants were economically poor, with little or no access to economic resources and job opportunities. They also had to deal with uncertainty and hostile receptions from the host communities. Later, many overseas Chinese also experienced discrimination and restrictions (although most of the discriminatory and restrictive practices now have been abolished). In North America, for example, many of the overseas Chinese who worked on railways in North America in the 19th century suffered from racial discrimination in Canada and the United States. Although discriminatory laws have been repealed or are no longer enforced today, both countries had at one time introduced statutes that barred Chinese from entering the country, for example, the United States Chinese Exclusion Act of 1882 (repealed in 1943) or the Canadian Chinese Immigration Act of 1923 (repealed in 1947).

In Southeast Asia, ethnic Chinese faced restrictions in countries such as Malaysia and Indonesia. In Malaysia, there are policies which give Bumiputeras (the Malays) privileges over other ethnicities. Such policies have lasted for about four decades, and are generally called *affirmative action*. Affirmative action is provided in the form of the Malaysian New Economic Policy or what is now known as the National Development Policy. Under this affirmative action policy, ethnic Malay are given many concessions, such as 70 percent of all of the seats in public universities, all initial public offerings (IPOs) must set aside a 30 percent share for

Bumiputera investors, and financial support is provided to Bumiputeras if they want to start their own businesses. Malaysian Chinese are considered "non-bumiputera" and hence cannot enjoy these concessions.

In Indonesia, in the new-order era under President Suharto, expressions of Chinese culture through language, religious activities, and traditional festivals were prohibited. Ethnic Chinese were encouraged to change their names into Indonesian names. In 1998, when Bacharuddin Jusuf Habibie became Indonesia's third president after Suharto resigned, he issued two presidential instructions. The first was the abolishment of the terms *pribumi* and *non-pribumi* (indigenous and non-indigenous) in official government documents and business. Second, the ban on the study of Mandarin Chinese was lifted. The 1996 instruction that abolished the use of the Indonesian Citizenship Certificate (*Surat Bukti Kewarganegaraan Republik Indonesia* or SKBRI) to identify citizens of Chinese descent was also reaffirmed. In 2000, Abdurrahman Wahid, the new president, abolished the ban on public displays of Chinese culture and allowed Chinese traditions to be practiced freely. Two years later, President Megawati Sukarnoputri declared that the Chinese New Year would be marked as a national holiday beginning in 2003. In 2006, the legislature passed a new citizenship law defining the word *asli* ("indigenous"), in the Constitution, as a natural-born person, allowing Chinese Indonesians to run for, and to be chosen as, president. The law further stipulates that children of foreigners born in Indonesia are eligible to apply for Indonesian citizenship.

Nevertheless, the discriminatory policies were limited only to politics. In economic and business areas, ethnic Chinese were still able to engage in their activities more freely. Many of them established new businesses, which would later play an important role in the economies of Malaysia and Indonesia.

Background of the Overseas Chinese Family Business (OCFB)

In every place they settled, Chinese immigrants always created a society where they could help each other. For example, they lent money to each other, since most of them were very poor. This money was used for specific purposes, such as establishing new businesses. The majority of overseas Chinese businesses are family owned, and family, knowledge, contacts, and trust are crucial.

Many OCFBs were able to develop beneficial relationships with their customers, local businesspersons, government institutions and officials, and people from outside the government. This enabled them to reduce cost and expand their businesses.

Most overseas Chinese family businesses diversified and expanded their business by following the development of products, services, and technology in the local, regional, and global market. These products, services, and technology were then adapted and offered to the local market, both in rural and urban areas, as well as to other countries. Many of them started with trade before diversifying to other sectors such as real estate, transportation, financial service, manufacturing, etc. Being involved in joint ventures and strategic partnerships with foreign companies helped OCFBs develop their global knowledge. They reinvested their growth surplus not only in the local market, but also in their country of origin and other countries.

Through collaboration and partnership, Chinese family businesses were also able to strengthen their position in specific markets. They did this by controlling manufacturing, trading, wholesaling, retailing, financing, and logistic activities. After earning enough money, the founders of Chinese family businesses send their children, who are expected to take over the businesses one day, to study in reputable higher institutions around the world. They hope their children will gain modern knowledge and skills that can be useful to the family business.

Strong bonds among Chinese communities in every place they settle have helped many OCFBs to flourish. Many of these businesses are grouped together, based on the market they serve, to strengthen the network and to exchange knowledge and resources.

Overseas Chinese Family Businesses in Southeast Asia

Overseas Chinese play an important role in Southeast Asian countries. In Indonesia, Chinese Indonesians own Indonesian private domestic capital.

In Malaysia, the Chinese comprise 30 percent of the population but control 50 percent of the total corporate assets. This is despite affirmative action policies which give Malays special privileges. In Thailand, Thai Chinese society plays an important role in business and politics (most Thai Prime Ministers are of Chinese origin). In the Philippines, Chinese Filipinos make up only 1 percent of the total Philippine population. Nevertheless, they control about 60 percent of the country's wealth.

As the colonialism era ended, Chinese Diasporas in Southeast Asia quickly began to fill the void in cross-border commerce. They capitalized on their access to cross-border capital, materials, labor, markets, and technology, mainly from Japan (Gupta, Graves, and Thomas, 2010). At the beginning, they structured their companies in a simple way, where the owner decided everything, as revealed by Redding (1995). They also only focused on one product that served one market, as well as built networks with customers, suppliers, and investors. Later, some of them diversified their businesses into unrelated sectors, becoming conglomerates that were united under the control of the family (Weidenbaum, 1996). Usually, in these kinds of businesses the husband and wife shared duties. The husband became the CEO, while the wife oversaw the financial operations by becoming the CFO (Tsang, 2001).

Starting in the 1970s, OCFBs evolved themselves. They did not only act as middlemen, but also started to build manufacturing companies as well. According to Weidenbaum (1996), thanks to their innovative nature, flexibility, high entrepreneurial skills, and spirits, they became the backbone of the Southeast Asian economy. They also created what was later known as the "bamboo network" (we will discuss the bamboo network in more detail in Chapter 8). Thanks to this network, which spread across Southeast Asia, the transaction cost could be reduced, exchanging information about business opportunities was easier, partnerships became more flexible, and barriers to trade could be minimized (Rauch and Trindade, 2002). When many western companies had to be restructured due to stiff competition from Japanese companies, these Chinese family businesses moved quickly to take benefits from such situations.

When the economic crisis hit the Southeast Asia economy in the late 1990s, many OCFBs in the region were badly affected.

As a result, they had to restructure their businesses. In addition, many of them also saw the crisis as an opportunity to prepare the younger generation so that they were ready to take over the businesses some day. The founders of Chinese family businesses, who had only limited formal education (some of them only finished elementary school), recognized the importance of education if they wanted their children, as well as their business, to move forward to deal with the new challenges.

Here are some prominent business families in the Southeast Asia region.

Indonesia

The Hartonos. Budi Hartono is from an old, established Chinese family in Kudus, Central Java, which controls P.T. Djarum Kudus, one of Indonesia's three major cigarette companies. Budi Hartono was chosen by his father—instead of his older brother, Michael Bambang Hartono—to run the business, but they continue to work together. In the 1970s, Budi diversified into electronic assembly, textiles, food processing, and banking. His son, Victor Rachmat Hartono, is the heir-apparent to the family business.

The Riadys. Mochtar Riady is the founder of Lippo Group. He was born on May 12, 1929, in Malang, East Java. The Lippo Group diversified its businesses into manufacturing, real estate, financial services (banking, investment, securities, insurance, asset management, and mutual funds), and infrastructure (power plants, gas production, roads, sanitation, and communication) sectors, which are largely handled by the Lippo Group Hong Kong office. In 1996, Lippo Group acquired 50 percent of retailer Matahari, owned by Hari Darmawan.

Mochtar's son, James, now runs the family business in Indonesia, while son Stephen takes care of their interests in Hong Kong.

The Widjajas. Eka Tjipta Widjaja was born in 1922 in China's Fujian province, the son of a trader based on the island of Sulawesi, and established the Sinar Mas Group, which specialized in plantations, pulp and paper, shipping, real estate, financial services, and much more. In the 1990s, he set up two pulp-and-paper companies in Jakarta, as well as Asia Pulp and Paper in New York. He was the controlling shareholder of Bank International Indonesia (which is currently owned by Maybank from Malaysia). Sinar Mas also controls Singapore's largest food company, Asia Food and Properties. During the Asian financial crisis, Sinar Mas lost its banking and other assets, while Asia Pulp and Paper managed a record emerging markets debt default of nearly US$14 billion in 2001. Despite this, the Widjajas retained control of their businesses. His four sons, Teguh, Indra, Muktar, and Franky, are the main managers of the family business today.

The Liems. Liem Sioe Liong's Indonesian name was Sudono Salim. He was born in Fuqing, Fujian province, in China in 1916, Liem Sioe Liong's father was a farmer, and he was the second son. He left Fujian in 1936 to join his brother, Liem Sioe Hie, and brother-in-law, Zheng Xusheng, in Medan, North Sumatra. Salim diversified their peanut oil trading business into the clove market, which was growing rapidly from demand for kretek production. He provided medical supplies to soldiers of the Indonesian National Revolution and met Suharto, an officer of the army, who later became Indonesia's second president. As Dutch businesses were taken over following Indonesia's independence, he acquired many of their assets. After moving to Jakarta in 1952, Salim expanded his trading business by cooperating with other ethnic Chinese businessmen in Singapore and Hong Kong. His soap factory became one of the primary suppliers to the Indonesian National Armed Forces (TNI). He later entered textile and banking businesses, eventually establishing the largest private bank in Indonesia, Bank Central Asia (BCA), in 1957. In 1968, he gained the right to a monopoly on clove importation. Together with his three best friends, namely Sudwikatmono, Ibrahim Risjad, and Djuhar Sutanto, Salim established Bogasari in 1970, which until now is Indonesia's largest flour producer. He also established the food manufacturing company, Indofood, which currently is the world's largest instant-noodle producer.

In 1992, Salim handed over management of the conglomerate Salim Group to his son, Anthony Salim. By 1997, the Salim Group possessed

US$20 billion in assets and included more than 500 companies employing over 200,000 workers. When the financial crisis hit Southeast Asia, the conglomerate was trapped by huge debt. Salim fled to Singapore during the May 1998 riots, when a mob burned his house in Jakarta. Nevertheless, his son stayed in Jakarta to rebuild the Salim Group. Salim died on June 11, 2012. He has four sons and one daughter and was once considered the richest individual in Indonesia.

Singapore

The Kweks. Kwek Hong Png was born in China in the early 1910s. He died in 1994. His business in construction materials began during World War II. The Kweks established a reputable Singapore land bank during the war and entered the real estate business before expanding into financial services in the 1960s. Today, Hong Png's businesses in Singapore are run by his son, Kwek Leng Beng, while Png's businesses in Malaysia are run by his nephew, Quek Leng Chan and his two brothers. The family's most famous companies include City Developments, Singapore Cement, and the Hong Leong Group.

The Wees. Wee Cho Yaw was born in 1929. He went to school in Singapore and England. Wee's father, Wee Kheng Chiang, sold pepper and rubber from Sarawak to Singapore, as well as ran an informal bank in Kuching. In 1935, Wee Kheng Chiang set up United Chinese Bank in Singapore. He asked his son to sit on the board of management in the 1950s, and soon after Wee Cho Yaw was handling the bank's daily operations. The bank grew rapidly in the 1960s and 1970s. In 1965, United Chinese Bank changed its name to United Overseas Bank (UOB). Wee Cho Yaw also entered the insurance, real estate, and hotel industries. Under Wee's leadership, the bank has become one of Asia's top banks, and continues to expand its presence locally and regionally.

The Lees. Lee Kong Chian built a hugely successful rubber business. He acquired plantations during the 1930s economic depression. Lee Rubber became the biggest plantation company in Southeast Asia. He was known as Southeast Asia's "Rubber and Pineapple King," and became one of the richest men in the region. Lee was born in the village of Furong of Nan'an City in Fujian, China. In 1903, when he was 10 years of age, he came to Singapore to join his father.

Lee facilitated the merger that later created Overseas Chinese Banking Corporation (OCBC) and became its first chairman. After World War II he became OCBC's largest shareholder. Lee Kong Chian died in 1967. His youngest son, Lee Seng Wee, succeeded his father. In 2003, Lee Seng Wee stepped down as chairman and moved to a non-executive position.

The Ngs. Ng Teng Fong was born in a small village in Putian, Fujian province, China. The eldest of 11 children, he came to Singapore with his family when he was just six years old. Ng's family owns the development corporations Far East Organization and Sino Group. Ng was known for his frugality. Though he owned and controlled at least a quarter of Singapore's housing market, Ng never moved from the house where he had lived for 30 years, and usually took his own lunch on airplanes. At the time of his death, Sino Group was one of Hong Kong's largest real estate developers, and Far East Organization remains one of the largest landholders in Singapore. Far East Organization also owns the Fullerton Hotel Singapore, a five-star luxury hotel, and numerous landmark hotels and other properties. His oldest son, Robert Ng, and younger son, Philip, are in charge of the family's interests in Hong Kong and Singapore, respectively. Ng died on February 2, 2010, at the age of 82.

Malaysia

The Kuoks. Robert Kuok Hock Nian was born in Johor in 1923. His father was a successful rice, flour, and sugar trader. After World War II ended, Kuok started his own business, by selling soft commodities and import substitutions. In the 1970s, he became known as "the sugar king" for his huge sugar trading deals and astute maneuvers in the London-based futures market. He diversified his business into other commodities such as flour and palm oil, as well as shipping, real estate, hotels, financial services, and much more. Kuok has changed his business home base several times, from Malaysia to Singapore to Hong Kong. Compared to his other peers, he is the most successful when doing business in different countries in Southeast Asia. Kuok has eight children from two marriages. Sons Beau and Chye, from his first marriage to Joyce Cheah, hold senior positions in his businesses, as do his nephews, Chye and Edward, and niece, Kaye.

Kuok's biggest source of wealth is Wilmar International, an agribusiness group that was established in 1991. It is one of the largest listed companies by market capitalization on the Singapore Stock Exchange. Wilmar International's business activities include oil palm cultivation, edible oils refining, oilseeds crushing, consumer pack edible oils processing and merchandising, specialty fats, oleo chemicals, biodiesel manufacturing, and grains processing and merchandising. In 2011, Wilmar International acquired Sucrogen, the world's fifth-largest sugar-refiner, from Australia.

The Yeohs. Francis Yeoh Sock Ping's family engaged in construction and the manufacturing of building materials. The family business, YTL, is named after Francis Yeoh's father, Yeoh Tiong Lay, who expanded it through early public works contracts after Malaysia gained its independence in the 1960s. Under Francis Yeoh's leadership, the YTL Group has grown into one of the biggest conglomerates in Malaysia. Among overseas assets, YTL owns Britain's Wessex Water Utility.

In 1996, YTL was the first Asian and non-Japanese company to list its shares on the Tokyo Stock Exchange. YTL has been named as one of the Top 250 Global Energy Companies in Asia under the Platts Top 250 Global Energy Company rankings. It also ranked 15th in the Fastest Growing Asian Companies.

Francis Yeoh's children are now involved in YTL. On January 16, 2003, Francis Yeoh was awarded the First Malaysian Ernst & Young Master Entrepreneur of the Year Award of 2002 in recognition of his achievements. He was also awarded *Business Week*'s "25 Stars of Asia 2003" in Hong Kong, and was ranked 21st by *Fortune* magazine's "Asia's 25 Most Powerful Business Personalities," on August 9, 2004.

Lee Shin Cheng Family. Lee Shin Cheng is the executive chairman of IOI Corporation Berhad (better known as the IOI Group). IOI, listed in Bursa Malaysia, is one of the world's leading conglomerates. Its businesses include oil palm plantations, specialty fats, oleo chemicals, and property development. IOI is also present outside Malaysia, in places such as Indonesia, the United States, and Europe. The IOI refinery in Rotterdam, the Netherlands, is the largest palm oil refinery in Europe. Lee has two sons and four daughters, who were all trained as lawyers. Lee and his family's control of IOI is held via Progressive Holdings Sdn. Bhd.

In recognition of Lee's contributions to the evolving needs and aspirations of the property industry in Malaysia, he was awarded "Property Man of the Year 2001" by FIABCI Malaysia. In February 2002, Universiti Putra Malaysia awarded Lee an Honorary Doctorate Degree in Agriculture in recognition of his contributions to the palm oil industry.

Vincent Tan Chee Yioun Family. He was born in 1952 in Batu Pahat, Johor, Malaysia. He worked as a clerk and an insurance agent before entering the business world in the 1980s. In 1982 he bought Malaysia's McDonald's franchise and in 1985 he bought Sports Toto when the government privatized the lottery agency. Currently, he owns Cardiff City FC, a football club from Wales, United Kingdom. He was also the chairman and chief executive of Berjaya Corporation Berhad (Berjaya), which specializes in property. He runs MiTV, the second pay-TV service in Malaysia, launched in September 2005. On February 23, 2012, Vincent Tan decided to retire from an active corporate role in Berjaya. He has handed over the CEO position to his son, Robin Tan.

The Philippines

The Gokongweis. John Gokongwei was born in Cebu in 1927. He came from a rich Chinese family. He traded clothes, scrap metal, and rice during the World War II. Later he expanded his business into food processing and mining. JG Summit is the name of his family conglomerate, which has interests in food processing, retailing, tele-communication, petrochemicals, real estate, shipping, and the airline Cebu Pacific Airways. From 2003 until now, his telecom company, Digital Telecommunications Philippines, has spent nearly $800 million for its mobile carrier, Sun Cellular, which was the third largest mobile operator in the Philippines as of 2008. Gokongwei also owns Universal Robina Corporation, one of the largest snack producers in the Philippines. He also controls Robinsons Land, one of the biggest property developers in the Philippines, which also operates a chain of malls.

His son, Lance Gokongwei is now in charge of the daily business activities. He leads the Gokongwei Empire, as president and COO, while his father serves as Chairman Emeritus.

The Tans (Asiaworld Group). Tan Yu was born to an ethnic Chinese copra trading family in Luzon in 1935. He built a textile manufacturing business after World War II, together with Jesus, his brother. He then set up a finance company, AIC Development, and invested in real estate around the region, especially in Taiwan. Because of his strong influence, the Taiwanese government was willing to bail out his local business in 1982. Two hundred hectares of prime land around Manila Bay became his important property asset. Its value reached its highest in the 1990s. He also created a large portfolio of real estate investments in Vancouver, Canada, and Texas. Tan died in 2002, and his daughter Emilia Roxas-Yang now leads Asiaworld Group.

The Yuchengcos. Enrique Yuchengco founded Chinese Insurance and Surety, later renamed Malayan Insurance Co., in 1930. He was a rich, second-generation Chinese lumber trader. His son, Alfonso, was born in 1923 and finished his studies at Columbia University. He succeeded in transforming Rizal Commercial Bank into a repu-table bank. He was also the main shareholder of Philippine Long-Distance Telephone (PLDT) and was its chairman until the mid-1990s. He diversified his business into other sectors such as infrastructure, pharmaceuticals, and so on. Several of his children work in the family businesses. Alfonso "Tito" Yuchengco III, the youngest child, is the most prominent.

Alfonso Yuchengco has been the Philippine Permanent Representative to the United Nations, with the rank of Ambassador Extraordinary and Plenipotentiary (AEP). He has also served as the Presidential Adviser on Foreign Affairs in 2004; Presidential Assistant on APEC Matters in 1998; Philippine Ambassador to Japan in 1995; Philippine Ambassador to China from 1986 to 1988; and Presidential Special Envoy to Greater China, Japan, and Korea. In 2005, President Gloria Macapagal Arroyo appointed Yuchengco as one of the members of the Consultative Commission for Charter Change, a special body tasked to study and recommend changes to the 1987 Philippines Constitution.

Andrew L. Tan Family. Tan was born in the Fujian province, China, and came from a humble family. He spent his childhood in an apartment in Hong Kong, which was shared by other families. He later moved to Manila and studied accounting at The University of The East. Since he did not have much money, he preferred walking to school instead of using public transportation. Currently, Andrew leads the Alliance Global Group Inc. (AGI). This was originally owned by George Yang, before it was handed to Andrew. AGI consists of three companies, namely Megaworld Corporation, Emperador Distillers Incorporation, and Golden Arches Development Corporation. Megaworld Corporation is a real estate corporation engaged in developing condominiums. *Finance Asia*, a business tabloid, awarded Megaworld Corporation "best managed company" and the "best in corporate governance" in the Philippines for 2006. Emperador Distillers Inc. produces and markets liquors and Golden Arches Development Corporation possesses a franchise of McDonald's. Andrew's son, Kevin, serves as Megaworld's first vice president. Megaworld is the first property developer in the Philippines that was awarded the ISO 9000 certification.

Thailand

The Chearavanonts. Dhanin Chearavanont inherited the agribusiness built up by his father, Chia Ek Chaw, and his uncle. Dhanin, who was born in 1939, transformed Charoen Pokphand (CP) into the largest agribusiness company in Thailand. Prior to the Asian economic crisis in 1997, CP was the largest conglomerate in Thailand. It expanded its business to many sectors such as telecommunications and automotive and became the biggest investor in China. After the Asian financial crisis, CP was forced to sell many of its assets in Thailand and China. Dhanin is helped by an elder brother and three sons.

The Sophonpanichs. Chin Sophonpanich was born in Bangkok in 1910. In 1952, he became the General Manager of Bangkok Bank, which was experiencing financial trouble at that time. His key political patron was General Phao Siryanon, director general of the Police. When Phao was ousted in a coup led by General Sarit Thanarat in 1957, Chin asked his lieutenants to be in charge. He lived in Hong Kong until Sarit died in 1963. When he was in exile, he worked hard to build networks outside Thailand. He also gave support, including financial assistance, to many businesspersons in Southeast Asia so that they could become more powerful. In the late 1980s and early 1990s Bangkok Bank had become the largest bank in Thailand. Chin died in 1988.

Chin's first son, Robin, took over the family businesses based in Hong Kong, while Chin's second son, Chatri, took over the businesses based in Thailand. When economic crisis struck Southeast Asia, Bangkok Bank was badly affected. As a result, the Sophonpanichs' control of the bank decreased. The biggest shareholder in the Bangkok bank is now a foreign company. Charti's son Chartsiri is the bank president.

The Chirathivats. The Chirathivats control the Central Group of Companies, a conglomerate holding company in Thailand that is involved in retailing, real estate, hotels, and restaurants. One of its subsidiaries is Central Pattana, the largest developer and operator of shopping centers in Thailand. Another subsidiary is Central Retail Corporation, Thailand's biggest retail conglomerate. Its main competitor is the Mall Group, which owns Siam Paragon, the Emporium, and several other shopping centers. Tiang Chirathivat built a merchandise store in 1947 in Samphanthawong district, a Chinatown in Bangkok. In 1957,

Tiang's son, Samrit Chirathivat, opened the first Central Department Store in Wangburapha, Phra Nakhon, Bangkok. The company's property development arm, Central Pattana, was founded in 1980, and opened its first shopping center, Central Plaza Lat Phrao, in Chatuchak district, Bangkok, in 1982.

The Ratanaraks. Krit Ratanarak was born in April 19, 1946. He is the Chairman of Bangkok Broadcasting and Television Company (BBTV) and leads one of the most prominent family business groups in Thailand. The Ratanarak family is the major shareholder in several Thai companies, such as Bank of Ayudhya, Siam City Cement, Ayudhya Allianz CP, Sri Ayudhya Capital, Matching Studio, Media of Medias, Eastern Star Real Estate, and BBTV. Krit took over the family businesses after his father, Chuan, died in 1993.

Chuan Ratanarak was born in 1920 in China. When he was six years old, his family moved to Thailand. In the 1940s Chuan started working on the docks in Bangkok. After he had enough money, he bought his own ship. He set up a shipping business, which flourished. Years after that, Chuan founded Bank of Ayudhya, Siam City Cement, and BBTV. By the 1980s Chuan's business had diversified into many sectors.

Krit joined Bank of Ayudhya in 1972. In 1982, he became the bank's president, and was named CEO in 1990. In 1993 he became Chairman and CEO of the Bank of Ayudhya, Chairman of BBTV, Chairman of Siam City Cement, and Chairman of Ayudhya Insurance. Krit helped the Bank of Ayudhya survive the Asian financial crisis in the late 1990s. As a result, the Ratanaraks became one of only eight companies that retained its position in Thailand's top 40 from 1979 to 2009. In 1999, Krit succeeded in gaining commitments from Holchim to invest its money and transfer its knowledge in Siam City Cement. In 2006, it was Bank of Ayudhya's turn to gain commitments from GE. Since 1993, Krit has added property companies Eastern Star and Grand Canal Land, as well as media company Matching Maximize Solution, to the family business group.

Krit's son, Chachchon Ratanarak, founded Tonson Group in 2006 and Tonson Property in 2007. They are the family's investment arm and property development businesses. Chachchon has been the director of Siam City Cement since 2007.

Overseas Chinese Family Businesses in Other Regions

The number and percentage of overseas Chinese living outside Southeast Asia is smaller, as well as their role in the economy. Nevertheless, we still can find some very large family businesses. One of them is the Li and Fung Group of Companies. Li and Fung is a trading company that supplies consumer goods. Garments make up around two-thirds of the Li and Fung business, which also covers the sourcing of hard goods such as fashion accessories, furnishings, gifts, handicrafts, home products, promotional merchandise, toys, sporting goods, and travel goods. The company was founded by Fung Pak Liu and Li To Ming. It is now led by two brothers, William and Victor Fung, the grandsons of Fung Pak Liu.

Another example is Marvell Technology Group Ltd. (Marvell). It is an American producer of storage, communications, and consumer semiconductor products. Founded in 1995, Marvell has operations around the world and employs about 5,700 workers. Marvell's U.S. operating headquarters is in Santa Clara, California. It also has international design centers in Europe, Israel, India, Singapore, and China. Outside the United States, Marvell has corporate offices in 16 countries. A leading fabless semiconductor company, Marvell sends over one billion chips a year. Marvell's expertise in microprocessor architecture and digital signal processing drives multiple platforms, including high-volume storage solutions, mobile and wireless, networking, consumer, and green products. Marvell was founded by Weili Dai, together with her husband, Dr. Sehat Sutardja, and her brother-in-law, Pantas Sutardja. All three are ethnic Chinese.

Another is Bing Lee, an Australian retailing company, a chain of superstores specializing in consumer electronics, computer, and telecommunication goods. Bing Lee is the largest electrical retail business in New South Wales. It has 41 stores. The company was founded by Bing Lee, a Chinese Australian, and his son, Ken Lee, in 1957. In the past, the source of the company's growth was the rising demand for televisions and other household items, such as washing machines, cooking equipment, heaters, and audio equipment. Bing Lee died in 1987 and his eldest son, Ken Lee, took over control of the business. Ken Lee died of cancer on December 21, 2007. His eldest son, Lionel Lee, took over as chief executive of the company.

Chapter 2

How Do Chinese Values Support Business Values?

The majority of Chinese enterprises, both on the mainland and overseas, are owned by families. A family business is a business where there is both significant family ownership and significant family involvement in management. A family business can be classified into *Family Owned Enterprise* (FOE) and *Family Business Enterprise* (FBE). FOEs are owned by family but managed by professionals. In the FOE, the family acts as the owner and assigns the responsibility of daily operations to professionals. With this separation of responsibilities, family members can optimize their role as supervisors. FBEs are owned and managed by the family members, who hold key positions in the enterprise. In the FBE, the family is involved in the company's daily operations and strategy formulation. Most Chinese family businesses are FBEs, but there are some FOEs among them.

In Chinese society, both on the mainland and overseas, Chinese culture exerts its influence on every aspect of life, including the way Chinese people conduct business.

The Role of the Family in Chinese Culture

The fact that there are many family-owned Chinese enterprises is not surprising since family culture is a tradition embedded in Chinese culture. Family is the core of Chinese ethics, traditions, and social organizations. Individuals are members of the family. According to the traditional Chinese education, promoting family ethos is seen as the most outstanding glory for an individual, and conversely, undermining them is one of the most unpardonable sins. In the family, parents are expected to educate their children and direct them toward a righteous life, whereas children should respect their parents, care for them, and protect their dignity. Family resources should be protected and enhanced to foster self-sufficiency (Efferin and Hopper, 2007). The founding of a family business is aimed at creating well-being for the whole family.

The value that takes family interests to be the most important end is known as *familism*. Familism has had a long history, during which the most effective rules—dealing with the relationships among family members, between family and society, and between family and state— have been stipulated. Familism was not only promoted by the rulers of every dynasty, financed by the esquires, and steered by academia; it was also propagandized by a variety of sacrifices and etiquettes, and even depicted in many plays and literary works. As a result, familism became the ethical standard for judging right and wrong, good and evil. This explains why Chinese people place a strong emphasis on family welfare—they always want to expand it and, along with it, glorify their ancestors. These factors make the Chinese work diligently and live frugally for the family, because frugality emphasizes saving, conserving resources, and displaying modesty.

In the Chinese community, accumulation of wealth has been identified as the standard for individual and family glory. Wealth is also the prime source of power as well as self-esteem and status. The

Chinese people are always ready to work long hours but still can maintain their enthusiasm. They never give up easily. They have a high degree of perseverance, patience, and quickness to act. They are patient enough to wait for the results, and seem to possess above-average endurance.

Confucian Values

Confucius is the most influential philosopher. Confucianism is not a religion. Instead, Confucianism is a set of guidelines for proper behavior. For hundreds of years, Confucianism has been actively taught and Confucian guidelines and manuals were written for all components of society. Confucian values are deeply rooted in Chinese society and families use stories, sayings, and terms to instill Confucian teachings in their children. The core of Confucianism is *humanism*, the belief that human beings are teachable, improvable, and perfectible through personal and communal endeavor, especially self-cultivation and self-creation. Confucianism focuses on the cultivation of virtue and maintenance of ethics.

According to Runes (1983), there are five virtues in Confucian ethics, namely *Ren* (humaneness), *Yi* (righteousness or justice), *Li* (propriety or etiquette), *Zhi* (knowledge), and *Xin* (integrity). They are accompanied by other elements such as *Zhong* (loyalty), *Xiao* (filial piety), *Cheng* (honesty), *Shu* (kindness and forgiveness), *Yong* (bravery), *Chi* (shame, judgement, sense of right and wrong), *Liang* (goodness, kindheartedness), *Gong* (respect, reverence), *Jian* (frugality), and *Rang* (modesty).

From all of the virtues, the three basics are *Ren*, *Yi*, and *Li*. *Ren* is an obligation of altruism and humaneness for other individuals within a community (Craig, 1998). *Altruism* is a concern for the welfare of others. Confucius' concept of humaneness is probably best expressed in the Confucian version of the ethic of reciprocity, or the *Golden Rule*: "Do not do unto others what you would not have them do unto you." Yan Hui, Confucius's most outstanding student, once asked his master to describe the rules of *Ren* and Confucius replied, "One should see nothing improper, hear nothing improper, say nothing improper, do nothing improper." *Yi* is the moral disposition to do good deeds. And *Li* consists of the norms of proper social behavior as taught to others by fathers, village elders, and government officials. The teachings of *Li* promoted ideals such as filial submission, brotherliness, righteousness, good faith, and loyalty. The influence of *Li* guided public expectations, such as loyalty to superiors and respect for elders in the community.

Confucius also identified four important qualities, namely education, commitment, collective responsibility, and mutuality and respect. Confucius also taught tolerance, harmony, solidarity, trustworthiness, contentedness, and conservatism.

According to Confucian teaching, there are five basic relationships. First, father and son: There should be kindness in the father, and filial piety in the son. Second, elder brother to younger brother: There should be gentility (politeness) in the elder brother, and humility in the younger. Third, husband and wife: The husband should be benevolent, and the wife should listen. Fourth, elder to junior: There should be consideration among the elders, and deference among the juniors. And fifth, ruler to the ruled: There should be benevolence among the rulers, and loyalty among the ruled.

Filial Piety

Filial piety means a high regard for older people, including parents and ancestors. It consists of being nice to parents and taking care of them; being good outside the home, in order to protect parents' and ancestors' good names; always doing the best job possible to give something to the parents; avoiding rebellion, loving, supporting, and respecting parents; building strong relationship among brothers; giving parents advice wisely; mourning the death of the parents; and carrying out sacrifices after they die. In many stories, filial piety is the main theme. Regardless of religious beliefs, which are varied among Chinese people, filial piety is commonly practiced.

Confucius once said: "In serving his parents, a filial son reveres them in daily life; he makes them happy while he nourishes them; he takes anxious care of them in sickness; he shows great sorrow over their death; and he sacrifices to them with solemnity." (Ikels, 2004). For Confucius, filial piety was not merely blind loyalty to parents. In other words, filial piety doesn't mean that fathers exploit their children without giving them anything in return. Children must show obedience and give support during the father's lifetime, as well as mourn his death. They must also do something better than their father has done. Nevertheless, a father must provide the best care, give the children the best education, and leave the children with a good name and reputation.

Guanxi

In Chinese organizations, continuing relationships are very important. These are in part based on family and other ties, such as clan, shared surname, home village, region, education, or other shared experience (Jacobs, 1980). In the Chinese community, *guanxi* is strongly empha-sized. *Guanxi* describes a personal connection between two people in which one is able to prevail upon another to perform a favor or service, or be prevailed upon. The two people need not be of equal social status. *Guanxi* can also be used to describe a network of contacts, which an individual can call upon when something needs to be done, and through which he or she can exert influence on behalf of another.

In *guanxi*, someone will get advantages because of his or her rela-tionships with family, friends, and other members of an organization. Chinese people have a tradition of expanding their network of *guanxi* relationships. Such relationships could last for the rest of life. Being part of a *gaunxi* does not mean that its members have mutual responsibilities, although failing to perform them is considered an unforgivable offense. We must note that when describing relationships among members of a family, such as father to son, the term *guanxi* is seldom, or even never, used. It is also seldom used to describe a relationship that has established norms, such as the relationship between students and teachers, or between managers and subordinates.

Characteristics of Chinese Family Businesses

The Chinese culture, such as familism, Confucian values, filial piety, and *guanxi* strongly influence the way the ethnic Chinese people do their business. The characteristics of most OCFBs include high cohesiveness, lack of organizational structure and rules, combining family ownership and management control, strong family relationship, early involvement of young generations, strong entrepreneurial skills and spirit, cost-consciousness, the promotion of glory and reputation, strong *guanxi* network, high dependency on patriarchs in resolving conflict, paternalistic leadership, and the passing down of values to the next generation.

High Cohesiveness

A high sense of cohesiveness within the hierarchy is commonly observed. A group, including a company, is said to be in a state of cohesion when its members possess bonds linking them to one another and to the group as a whole.

One example is Panda Express. Panda Express is a fast casual restaurant chain serving American Chinese cuisine. It operates mainly inside the United States and is the largest chain of Chinese fast-food restaurants in the United States. Panda Express has proved itself to be an effective competitor against larger corporate fast-food chains such as McDonald's, KFC, and Taco Bell, and thousands of other independent rivals.

The chain offers a variety of entrees such as Orange Chicken, Beijing Beef, Mandarin Chicken, and Kung Pao Chicken. Combo meals are served with fried rice, steamed rice, chow mein, or mixed vegetables. No MSG is added to any of the items at Panda Express after it has been delivered to the restaurant, nor does Panda Express purchase from any suppliers who add MSG prior to delivery.

Andrew Cherng opened the first Panda Inn in Pasadena, California, with his father, Master Chef Ming-Tsai Cherng, in 1973. Panda Inn was one of the first restaurants to introduce the robust flavors of Mandarin and Szechuan cuisine to Southern California. In 1983, after the success of Panda Inn, Andrew Cherng opened the first Panda Express. The restaurant is located in the Glendale Galleria in California, and is a pioneer in the quick-service Chinese food market. It quickly became the Chinese food of choice for consumers and developers. In 1992, they also established the first Hibachi-San Japanese Grill in the Mall of America in Bloomington, Minnesota. Today, Panda Inn, Panda Express, and Hibachi-San are under the parent company Panda Restaurant Group. The group has its headquarters in Rosemead, California.

Andrew Cherng says Panda Express restaurants are successful because he cares about the emotional well-being of the employees. Cherng and his managers inquire about employees' personal lives, hobbies, spiritual beliefs, and relationships with family. Cherng, who says he can't expect people to do a good job at work if their lives are a mess, preaches self-improvement through meditation, education, and fulfilling hobbies. His monthly Saturday morning personal wellness seminars draw 100 or so employees to hear about nutrition, intimacy, and self-awareness. He encourages managers in the company's L.A. corporate office and in company-owned restaurants to forge personal bonds with their employees by devoting several hours a week to chats about spirituality, effective parenting, and personal ambitions. What Cherng does is similar to what the Riadys do in Indonesia, with their Thursday prayers led by the owners.

Cherng's managers are encouraged to come up with get-to-know-you gatherings outside Panda's offices and restaurants, which also include Panda Inn and Hibachi-San. One tries to have quarterly bowling matches. Another holds a jump-rope class. Yet another took workers on a 25-mile hike. "You can't expect someone to do a good job if you treat them like an object," Cherng says.

In OCFBs, if possible, the subordinates should not express them-selves and show their self-interest publicly. The cordial relationships and high tolerance among fellow members in the Chinese enterprise have become part of the dynamics of relationship management (Wah, 2001). Seniority, reliability, and trustworthiness play a more important role in deciding promotion, hiring, firing, rewards, and evaluation criteria instead of good performance.

Lack of Formal Organizational Structure and Rules

In practice, many Chinese family businesses do not have a formal organizational structure, which implies that the management position is based on the individual position and seniority in the family hierarchy (Wah, 2001). The organizational chart does not necessarily provide information about who actually holds the power. Often a person with an influential-sounding title may be only a figurehead. In terms of structuring of activities, there is low specialization of task with practically no clear job descriptions and work procedures. Moreover, reporting relationships are interchangeable, thus resulting in role conflicts. Lower-level managers or employees often can go straight to their leaders or superiors without going up through the chain of command. In the Chinese family businesses, there is hardly any formulation of written policies and rules. This is because they tend to believe in collective responsibility. Although roles are not specifically written, Chinese family business leaders have high expectations of the subordinates' good conduct of behavior such as obedience, reliability, and trustworthiness.

In many Chinese family businesses, strategies and decisions are often made on the basis of experience, intuition, and informality. Decision-making is informal and often occurs at events such as family dinners, family breakfasts, or even family holidays.

Combining Family Ownership and Management Control

Today, many Chinese family businesses continue to reflect a family-oriented structure, in which individual members of the controlling family still play a key role. This continues even after the company goes public. A number of large enterprises, for example, manage the transition from a traditional to a relatively modern business structure by installing the sons and daughters who graduated from the best schools around the world. In this way, the family retains ultimate control but applies modern Western management techniques to improve the company.

In many Chinese family businesses, family ownership and management are often combined. Such combination partially results both from low trust in outside professionals and from reliance on trust built through kinship or personal relationship (Yan and Sorensen, 2006).

Keeping management and ownership within the family reduces some of the agency problems in publicly listed corporations and FOEs. Agency problem is a conflict of interest arising between shareholders and management because of differing goals. For example, an agency problem exists when management and stockholders have conflicting ideas on how the company should be run.

Strong Family Relationships

Family members have a deep understanding and trust among themselves. Family enterprise can also easily get a full commitment from the employees. These employees sometimes are even willing to compromise their salaries. The understanding, trust, and commitment among family members and employees make the information flow easily.

As a result of familism, many Chinese family businesses prefer recruiting family members and relatives into the company. For example, we can see the case of Lee Kuai Lim or K.L. Lim (1877−1936). In his early twenties, he started his business by opening a silk trading firm called Kam Lun Tai, in his hometown, Zhenlong, China. His business acumen made the silk trading a great success. Soon afterward, he earned his first bucket of gold and opened branches in Xinyi, Huazhou, Dianbai, and even further to the capital city of Zhanjiang in Southern Guangdong Province. In each of these branches, he deployed family members, such as uncles, brothers, or cousins, to supervise the daily operation. That kind of management mechanism seemed efficient and his business prospered. Parallel to his wealth accumulation, his business connections also spread radically and rapidly. In 1899, he expanded his silk trading network outward to Hong Kong by buying a shop on Connaught Road Central where Nam Pak Hong, the business center in the Colony, was located.

When he later learned that there was a high demand for Chinese silk in Southeast Asia, he went there. In 1903, he set up branches in Kuala Lumpur and Singapore. His frequent travels to these places led him to other, bigger business opportunities. Several months later, recommended by one of his clients, K.L. Lee bought an ore field in Malaya and decided to step into the tin mining business. He gave the newly set-up company the name "Tai Yau," meaning it was a subsidiary of Kam Lun Tai. Later, K.L. Lee diversified his business into what we would now call human resources, lodging, money changing, and remittance. Unfortunately, after K.L. Lim died in 1936, Kam Lun Tai faded due to external factors and leadership continuity problems. H.S. Lee, son of K.L. Lee, who was assigned by his father to take charge of the family business, was more interested in pursuing his political career in Malaysia. K.L. Lee did not assign any position in the family business to his two youngest sons.

Early Involvement of the Younger Generation

The children of Chinese family business leaders often start their involvement in the business by doing an internship. For example, Nyonya Meneer, the founder of the company with the same name, now one of Indonesia's biggest traditional medicine companies, appointed two of her daughters to mind the shop after school. The children's involvement with the company started early in their life and they knew that their whole life depended on the business. If the business does not succeed, the family will not survive. Thus, they are committed to do their best both for the family and the company. The commitment is even higher since they know that their parents want them to take over the business management someday. This younger generation also tries to prove to their parents that they have the same competencies and abilities as their parents did in managing the business. The younger generation of the family may not have been working for the company as long as their parents but they have the sense of ownership that encourages them to work hard. They are emotionally attached to the company, thus the sense of kinship among them is very strong, which influences the dynamic within the family.

Early involvement in the business helps children develop their entrepreneurial skills and spirit, although this doesn't necessarily mean that they will continue their parents' business. Ciputra, the founder of Ciputra Group in Indonesia, is one example. His father owned a grocery store in Central Sulawesi, Indonesia. When he was a little child, he helped his parents. He was used to seeing merchandise and was involved in the business transactions. He was surrounded with the business environment for 24 hours a day. So, it was not surprising that his business instinct had been continually developed. His father died when Ciputra was 12 years old. Before the age of 30, he was able to build a joint venture with the local government to turn a swamp area into a theme park, the first in Indonesia.

Strong Entrepreneurial Skills and Spirit

The characteristics of people with strong entrepreneurial skills include adaptability, willingness to compete with others, self-confidence, discipline, strong motivation, honesty, persistence, persuasiveness, readiness to take risk, empathy, creativity, and clear vision for the business. All of these characteristics are inherent in Chinese family business owners.

Sudono Salim is a good example of a person with strong entrepreneurial skills. He, like any other ethnic Chinese person, is very good in maintaining trust, is a hardworking person, and is also humble although very successful in his business. His humility can be seen from his office, his residence, and his lifestyle. He also stresses the importance of getting an education.

Salim also had a strong vision in developing one of the best banks in Indonesia, the Bank Central Asia (BCA). Although he had to give up his ownership in BCA due to the economic crisis in the late 1990s, there is no doubt that he has been successful in building a strong foundation for the bank.

The overseas Chinese entrepreneurs are dynamic and resilient. This will help them survive in a competitive business environment. They are able and willing to serve a large number of customers simultaneously. This will in turn create efficiency and foster good relationships with customers.

Overseas Chinese entrepreneurs are well-known for their patience and impulsiveness. They always wait for upcoming opportunities and then take benefits from those opportunities immediately. They are flexible and set targets based on the actual conditions. They are willing to change and adapt to business situations and make sure that everything will run smoothly. These things are done in order to increase their self-confidence. They are also willing to learn new cultures.

Many Chinese family business leaders are good in identifying and exploiting business opportunities and have high entrepreneurial skills (Wah, 2001). Sudono Salim, the founder of Salim Group, Indonesia's biggest conglomerate, is well-known for these skills. A person who knows him well explained Salim's move to the automotive industry. At the time, Japanese motor vehicles were the best; Yamaha was already taken and Honda was part of Astra. But, Suzuki was part of a local company. Salim talked to the Suzuki sole agency holder in order to ask him to cooperate, but he refused. He did, however, want to sell his business at a very high price. In terms of return on investment, it was too high, but Salim agreed to buy it. It was very expensive, US$50 million or so at the time. Suzuki went on to become number-two in the market in Indonesia.

Currently, Salim has expanded their business globally. The group has made investments in more than 40 countries. The money invested is controlled through their Hong Kong–based company, First Pacific Company Limited, which was established in 1981. The company's assets have grown steadily, from US$1.8 billion in 2011 to US$7.88 billion at the end of 2011. One of the biggest investments is in the Philippines, through their ownership of Philippine Long-Distance Telephone Company and Metro Pacific Investments Corporation.

Another example is Dhanin Chearavanont from CP, Thailand. Dhanin entered the Chinese market right from the beginning. To build a feed mill and poultry farm, he won "Foreign Investor Certificate No. 001" in 1979, just after Deng Xiaoping launched his economic reforms. Dozens more followed, and for decades CP was ranked as China's biggest foreign investor. Today half of CP's sales are generated in China.

In 2005, China began overhauling its agricultural sector. The goal was to move to bigger and more efficient farms, and CP was quick to seize the new opportunities. The company mobilized more than US$10 billion in bank credit, government support, and its own funds to develop cutting-edge projects that would produce vast quantities of eggs, poultry, and produce each year. These carefully laid plans culminated in April 2005 with the opening of an automated egg factory near Beijing that produces 840 million eggs a year. Later, a $1.2 billion farm in Zhanjiang City, Guangdong Province began raising 100 million broiler chickens and 1 million pigs a year. Other farms are under construction or planned in Zhejiang, Jilin, Xinjiang, Liaoning, and Tianjin.

Ciputra from Indonesia is another example of how a Chinese family business has shown great entrepreneurial skills. Soon after graduating from college, he was able to meet and then convince the Governor of

Jakarta, at that time Soemarno, to establish a joint venture to build the Pasar Senen Project. Soemarno then asked another businessman, Hasjim Ning, Medi Foundation, and Bumi Putera Foundation to establish Perseroan Terbatas (PT) Pembangunan Jaya (currently known as Jaya Group). Ciputra became the CEO of the company and held the position until 1995. Since the beginning, Ciputra believed that this business idea had a bright future that would last for many years to come.

Now let's take a look at Panda Express. One of the secrets that made Andrew Cherng's Panda Express a success story was being open to new opportunities. Not a big shopper, Andrew Cherng rarely visited malls. However, he felt interested after hearing a suggestion from one of his regular customers, who at that time was developing a new mall near Los Angeles. The customer said that many people would come to Cherng's restaurant if Cherng opened it in the mall. Until that time, no Chinese restaurant had done that. Nevertheless, Cherng followed his friend's advice.

Cherng also saw an opportunity to offer something different compared to his competitors. While other restaurants such as McDonald's and KFC offered white meat chicken nuggets, Cherg saw that the dark meat, as one part the chicken, was rarely offered. As a result, he could buy his meat at a lower price. He could also serve chicken that was moister because the fat content was higher.

Recently, Panda has established a new company, Panda Dry Cleaning. For the next five years, The Cherng family intends to add up to 200 standardized shops across the country. Tide Dry Cleaners is the franchised shop that was opened in Henderson, the suburb of Las Vegas. In 2012, Panda planned to increase the presence of Tide Dry Cleaners by opening at least five more shops. Many of the shops will be established in California. This industry does not have any established players, like McDonald's or KFC in the fast food industry. Hence, Cherng saw this as the chance to expand the business.

Andrew Tan from the Philippines once said, "My philosophy as a businessman is really quite simple: Just keep working and investing whatever profit you make in new businesses. That way, you generate more jobs and help the country's economy grow. I, for one, spend most of my time working. For that reason, I don't get to spend money that much. After all, you also need time to spend your money."

Cost-Conscious

A Chinese entrepreneur sees the business as an empire that will be inherited by his children (Redding, 1982). Based on this rationale, the Chinese entrepreneurs normally reinvest their earnings. In other words, they will always spend the money carefully. This is done to ensure that the business is in a healthy condition and has enough money by the time the children take it over. Many of them are also ready to sacrifice short-term financial profit to achieve sustainable growth and development in the future. In other words, many Chinese family businesses are cost-conscious. This cost-consciousness is reflected in the low margin and high volume of products in penetrating markets, rigorous control on inventory to achieve low capital investments, and the reduction of costs of doing business. This cost-conscious behavior might also be inspired by the Confucian teaching of frugality.

Promoting Glory and Reputation

The emphasis on promoting glory and reputation for the family and business has made Chinese people work diligently and live frugally. This has contributed very much to the early successes of overseas Chinese family businesses, although they are also very motivated to maintain a good living. Family members realized that, with limited capital, only by working hard together could they find a way to survive.

Sudono Salim can be regarded as someone working for *Fu Lu Shou*, which refers to the concepts of good fortune (*Fu*), prosperity (*Lu*), and longevity (*Shou*). In fact, it has become the goal of many Chinese people, including the Chinese family business.

In many cases, the company's brand name and its products greatly influence the family identity. Therefore, if the company's product is perceived to have low quality, it is considered a reflection on the family.

This is another reason why family businesses are not interested in pursuing short-term financial gain and why they always focus on quality. When Charoen Pokphand (CP) was first being established, the agricultural industry in Thailand and the region was still at a novel stage. Many firms exploited the unregulated market environment by mixing other substances into their animal food in order to increase quantity. But the founder of CP told his sons that they, on the other hand, will stick to quality: "CP produces animal food not for puppies or goldfish lovers. Our customers are farmers. If they cannot survive because their animals are not healthy, neither can we." With the focus on quality, CP became very successful within a short time. Today, the company has grown into a global business, with more than 250 subsidiaries in 20 countries, including China. CP is now the fifth-largest feed-mill operator in the world. The CP's current CEO, Dhanin Chearavanont, is the son of the founder.

Another example is Panda Express. Tom Davin, the company's CEO from 2004 to 2009, once pressed Andrew Cherng to sell franchises, telling him the company could have 10,000 stores in a few years. No thanks, says Cherng. He doesn't trust independent owners to continue his work of breaking down the traditional barriers between employees' work lives and personal lives.

Promoting family and business reputation is also done through social activities. Many of them set up an institute or foundation. Take Mochtar Riady, for example. He set up the Mochtar Riady, Institute of Nanotechnology (MRIN) in 2008. The MRIN was founded with the aim to conduct innovative cancer research, to help understand the association of gene mutation or changes with cancer development in Indonesian patients.

In Malaysia, Robert Kuok founded the Kuok Foundation. The Kuok Foundation was set up by the Kuok family in 1970 to alleviate poverty and to reduce the economic disparities between the rich and poor communities in Malaysia. The foundation's activities include the advancement of education and the alleviation of poverty through education, providing funding for social and welfare activities undertaken by NGOs and other nonprofit organizations, job placement programs, get-togethers for Kuok Foundation Awardees, and Scholars' Reunion Dinners.

In the Philippines, John Gokongwei set up Gokongwei Brothers Foundation (GBF) in 1992 to help raise the socioeconomic condition of Filipinos through the funding of educational projects. The first of these was the Technical Training Center for skilled graduates in various engineering fields. A significant endowment by the foundation to the Ateneo de Manila University then led to the John Gokongwei School of Management (JGSOM), a regional powerhouse in the field of management education. It has also aggressively donated facilities and scholarships, and supported educational programs to help train the next generation of business and government leaders in schools such as Immaculate Concepcion Academy, Xavier School, De La Salle University, the University of Asia and the Pacific, and the University of San Carlos.

In Singapore, Lee Kong Chian set up the Lee Foundation in 1952. It is a charitable foundation created to aid in "the advancement of education, medicine and cultural activities; helping the poor; and assisting victims of fire, flood and famine." It also funded other philanthropic work. In 1957, Lee Seng Gee took over from his father as chairman of the foundation.

The Role of Guanxi

Guanxi is necessary to ensure that Chinese family businesses can operate reliably. According to Chen (2001), *guanxi* networks are valuable sources of information on issues for which official channels are inadequate. In a society in which laws are not enforced uniformly, *guanxi* networks help businesses deal with one another. The closest relationships are those of the immediate family. After that, the next closest are the extended family and very close friends who are treated as family. Such close friends do not have to be Chinese to be considered an insider. The next level of relationship is that between people with shared experiences, such as former classmates. The final level of relationship is that with strangers, who often are looked upon with suspicion until they are known better. *Guanxi* relationships often result in favors that are expected to be returned, but by no specific date. Sometimes indebtedness from such favors lasts for generations, and the Chinese will remember for a long time a favor that was granted them when it was especially needed. It is important to note that *guanxi* networks are among individuals and not companies. When a person leaves a position, his replacement does not inherit the network. Sometimes companies will appoint the replacement far in advance so that he can be introduced to the network. *Guanxi* relationships should be maintained through a steady exchange of communication and favors. A failed business deal does not mean the end of a *guanxi* relationship. Rather, it often strengthens it since surviving difficult times helps to bring people closer together. The Chinese consider adversity to be the best test of a relationship.

Let us again take a look at Kam Lun Tai under the leadership of K.L. Lee. When he opened his tin mining business in Malaya, the supply of cheap labors was limited. This forced K.L. Lee to redefine his business plan and it quickly reminded him that there indeed were lots of villagers left unemployed in his hometown. If he could import the unemployed labor from China, he not only could solve the labor shortage in Malaya but could help his fellow villagers make a living.

He told his uncle, Lee Lan-Kiu, and his younger brother, Lee Yu-Kam, who were key persons in managing business in China, about the situation in Malaya and his idea about exporting labor. Although he gained full support from most of his family members, he had to persuade the French government—at that time Zhanjiang was one of the French concessions in China—to allow him to export the labor (Fung, 1984). Seeing K.L. Lee's proposal could release socioeconomic pressure from the administration, the French government responded positively. By the end of 1904, with the blessing from the authorities, K.L. Lee started to recruit labor in Zhenlong.

Guanxi can ensure a higher level of trust and thus lower the cost of transactions. However, according to Charles Saerang, the president director of Nyonya Meneer—one of the biggest herbal companies in Indonesia—building friendships and networks takes time. Nothing is instantaneous.

Sudono Salim is an overseas Chinese family businessperson who is very good at maintaining his *guanxi* network. His friendships with his business associates are legendary. He often solves a complex business problem while at the same time maintaining good relationships with his partners. Once there was a disagreement between Salim's second generation and the second generation of his business associates,

Sudwikatmono, Ibrahim Risjad, and Djuhar Sutanto. There were some assets used to pay the debt. Each side made a claim. For Salim, he could solve such a problem easily. It would be solved based on trust.

High Dependency on Patriarchs or Matriarchs

In many Chinese family businesses, potential conflicts are often mediated and resolved by the patriarchs as long as they are still in full control of the business and the family. Therefore, conflicts seldom emerge. Even if they do, they often avoid shaking the foundation of trust among family members. This is because the patriarchs or matriarchs have the final say regarding business policies and activities, particularly regarding strategic issues.

Conflicts often emerge after the patriarchs, particularly the first generation leader, pass away. This was the case in Nyonya Meneer, as well as in Yeo Hiap Seng (YHS), a food and beverage manufacturer based in Singapore. In Nyonya Meneer, conflicts broke out among Nyonya Meneer's children and grandchildren, while in YHS, conflicts in the family emerged after the third generation joined the company. Conflicts in both companies arose from disagreement in managing the family firms. We will learn more about conflicts in family businesses in Chapter 4.

Paternalistic Leadership

In paternalistic leadership, leaders give more attention to the social needs and views of their workers. Leaders are interested in how happy workers feel, and in many ways act as father figures. They consult with employees over issues and listen to their feedback or opinions. The leaders will, however, make the actual decisions (in the best interests of the workers) as they believe the staff members still need direction. In many Chinese family businesses, family firm leaders are often patriarchs who have full control over the company and business.

Paternalistic leadership enhances efficiency in the decision-making process, in both business and family issues. Founder and family members make decisions regarding strategic issues, since there's an assumption that they are in a better position than the employees to know what is best for the organization. With frequent communication and conformity to authority, family members can easily come to a consensus or reach an agreement. This helps to enforce and implement decisions more quickly and effectively, without bureaucracy. Paternalistic leadership also fosters organization adaptability, harmony, compliant and diligent subordinates, and stable organizational membership.

Passing Down the Cultural Values

Chinese family business leaders pass down the Chinese cultural values such as frugality, trustworthiness, harmony, education, diligence, patience, and perseverance to the next generation. They believe that such values are proven to support business growth and development. One example is Kwek Hong Png. He was the founder of Hong Leong, one of the biggest Chinese conglomerates in Asia, based in Singapore. He placed high importance on the value of education and professional training. Both his sons had overseas university educations. The elder, Kwek Leng Beng, graduated as a lawyer from the University of London and the younger, Kwek Leng Joo, graduated in business from a university in Japan. This is typical for many Chinese family business leader—sending their children to study abroad, particularly to western countries. Many of the younger generation graduated from the best schools in the world. Another example is Qian Hu. Qian Hu is engaged in the import and export, farming and distribution of ornamental fish, as well as the distribution of aquarium and pet accessories. One of Singapore's two top exporters of ornamental fish, Qian Hu exports directly to more than 45 countries. Yap Tik Huay, the founder of Qian Hu, passed critical values down to his children, Executive Chairman Kenny Yap and his four brothers. These shaped the management culture of today's family business. Those values include: integrity, diligence, loyalty, trust, respect, teamwork, and family unity. Chinese cultural values are passed down not only to the children, but to staff as well.

Charles Saerang from Nyonya Meneer, in one interview, said that values imposed were honesty, persistence, and diligence. However, the younger generation have the opportunity to choose and decide their future. Children must also create networks through education. Selection of a university and friends becomes the focal point of the parents' role.

Husodo Angkosubroto from Gunung Sewu, an Indonesian conglomerate specializing in property, agribusiness, manufacturing, and subsequently financial services and telecommunications, emphasizes values such as hard work, obligation to the family and company, and submission to the elderly.

Kevin Tan, the son of Andrew Tan from the Alliance Global Group Inc., Philippines, said that his father taught him to be compassionate, patient, and diligent, as well as to keep his focus and always be generous to others. Kevin sums up the priceless lessons he learned from his father: "Nothing in this world comes for free or without sacrifice. You can never take a shortcut to anything. If you want to succeed, you must work harder than the rest, keep your determination and focus, and be creative and innovative. My dad also always reminds me to give back firstly to the thousands of people who work for us, and secondly to charity. Taking care of people, especially those who work for us is one of the most important things to do. Generosity is a very important virtue that my dad has inculcated in all of us."

In a recent interview, Michael Widjaja, the grandson of Eka Tjipta Widjaja, the founder of Sinarmas, said Sinarmas Land, one of the subsidiaries of Sinarmas, continues the values instilled by Eka Tjipta. The first of those values is triggered by customers, because the business starts and ends with customers. Therefore, it is important to understand trends and behavior, and to be involved in every way. Second is integrity. Integrity means without compromise—honest, reliable, and responsible. Third is innovation. Innovation must be done continuously, supported by aggressive research and advanced technology. Fourth is unity. This means people in the company should have quality and mutual trust, support each other, be dependable, and have a high sense of belonging. And fifth is diligence. This means that employees must never stop learning, continuously improve, and be persistent.

Challenges Facing Overseas Chinese Family Businesses

As the family business grows and the environment changes, both externally and internally, some traditional practices in OCFBs face great challenges. Here are some challenges that should be anticipated.

Managing Growth

All business owners aspire to grow their companies. Growth in a company is indicated with the increase in terms of assets, revenue, profit, market size, number of products and services, employees, factories, outlets, branches, operation locations, and so on. As the company grows, more professionals outside of the family are needed, since the skills and knowledge of family members regarding products, technology, market, and management will no longer be sufficient.

Different markets, products, or services require different approaches. In such a situation, the family business needs people who have better experience, skills, and knowledge regarding a certain market or product. It also needs people with a wide network. Often such qualifications can be met only by people outside of the family.

Requirements for specialty, advanced technology, competence, organization structure, and system will also become much higher. It becomes more difficult for the business to supervise the company only with family members; they have to delegate some authority and responsibility to outsiders.

Globalization

Globalization refers to the process or processes of international integration. Globalization means there are no boundaries regarding time and place. Free trade allows the products, services, and resources to move freely across countries and regions without any barrier. Many rules and regulations that hinder business competition and flow of goods, services, and capital should be abolished. Today, many countries have signed free trade agreements, both bilaterally and regionally. For example, ASEAN and China signed a free trade area with the intent of establishing a free trade area among the 11 nations by 2010. The free trade area came into effect on January 1, 2010.

Rapid Development of Information and Communication Technology (ICT)

With the rapid development of ICT, people can access more information very quickly at any time and any place. The access to ICT today is becoming easier, cheaper, and faster. As a result, every day we receive abundant information and opinions with different kinds of perspective. Abundant information and opinions also provide more insight and alternatives for problem solving in all aspects of life, including in business areas.

Increasing Competition

Today, a company must compete not only with other companies within the same industry, but also with other industries—not only with companies in the same country and region, but from different countries and regions as well. Increasing competition means that companies must promote creativity and innovation. Therefore, the entrepreneurial spirit in the family business should be maintained. Such a spirit has also made many OCFBs more resilient in dealing with various challenges, including external crises. Their long lifespan reflects their success in overcoming various crises, not only economic but also political and social crises as well. In Indonesia, the three examples that are able to survive from one crisis to another are herbs, tobacco, and food and beverage. Some of the oldest herb companies in Indonesia are Nyonya Meneer (founded in 1918), Jamu Iboe (1910), and Jamu Jago (1918). In the tobacco industry, we have Bentoel (founded in 1930, acquired by British American Tobacco or BAT in 2010), Djarum (1951), and Gudang Garam (1958). In the food and beverage industries, we have Sosro (founded in 1940) and Khong Guan (1970).

The Growing Influence of Generation Y

The influence of Generation Y is growing significantly. This should be considered since it poses challenges to the traditional practices of

Chinese family business. This generation was born in the mid-1970s and later. They grew up in the middle of ICT rapid development. They are smarter, more creative, more critical, and more demanding. They usually demand a clearer career path, with more opportunities for personal and career development and bigger compensation. They also demand more work—life balance. Today, young people freely move from one company to another in order to seek better compensation and career development.

Chapter 3

Combining Modern Management and Chinese Traditional Values

C hinese traditional values, which emphasize family relation and glory, education for younger generations, seniority, collective responsibility, harmony, magnanimity, diligence, hard work, trustworthiness, and solidarity translate into the family business. In most overseas Chinese family businesses (OCFBs), the ownership and involvement of family members is significant. They make strategic business decisions, develop business strategies, and oversee the company's daily activities.

Family Businesses around the World: An Overview

Family businesses play a significant role in many parts of the economies of both developed and developing countries. Based on the data from

45

Family Firm Institute (FFI), family businesses create an estimated 70 to 90 percent of global Gross Domestic Product (GDP) annually.

In Canada, around half of the country's workforce is employed by a family business, creating nearly 45 percent of Canadian GDP. In the United States (U.S.), the biggest economy in the world, the greatest part of America's wealth lies with family owned businesses. According to Astrachan and Shanker (2003), family firms comprise 80 to 90 percent of all business enterprises in North America. Family businesses also employ about 62 percent of the U.S. workforce. Some prominent names include Ford Motor Company, Wal-Mart, Hilton, and the Marriott Corporation.

In Brazil, Latin America's biggest economy, the majority of businesses in the country are family owned. Family firms represent 70 percent of the largest Brazilian business groups. In Chile, it is estimated that between 75 to 90 percent of all the firms in the country are family owned and controlled. Roughly 65 percent of the medium- to large-size enterprises in Chile are family owned. Chile's family owned businesses are typically well-organized corporate entities with decentralized command structures and little day-to-day control by individual shareholders.

In Europe, family businesses also play important role in big economies such as Germany, France, the United Kingdom (U.K.), Spain, and Italy, as well as smaller economies such as Austria, Denmark, Ireland, Norway, Portugal, and Sweden. The situation in former communist countries in Eastern Europe such as Czech Republic, Estonia, Hungary, Latvia, Slovenia, and Slovakia is no different. In almost all European countries, more than half of the businesses are owned and/or controlled by families. Some prominent family businesses from Europe include BMW, Henkel, Merck (Germany); L'Oreal (France); FIAT, Parmalat (Italy); H&M (Sweden); Lego (Denmark); Sainsburys (UK); and Camper (Spain).

Around 75 percent of the Middle East's private economy is controlled by 5,000 high-net-worth families, with their companies creating 70 percent of the region's employment. Family businesses control over 90 percent of commercial activity. In Turkey, 90 percent of Turkish businesses constitute family firms. Sabanci Holding, the largest industrial and financial conglomerate in Turkey by profit, is one of the most prominent family businesses in Turkey.

In Australia, 67 percent of the companies in the country are family businesses, in which 90 percent of them employ less than 200 people

(Thomas, 2006). In 60 percent of the Australian family owned companies, the owning families are directly involved.

Currently, the oldest family business in the world, Houshi Onsen, is operating in Japan and is managed by the 46th generation of the founding family, according to Barclays Wealth and *The Economist* Intelligence Unit (2009). The longevity of Japanese family companies may be attributed to the practice of turning sons-in-law into true family insiders, thereby broadening the pool for successors and talented managers without involving non-family members. Family businesses tend to outperform non-family companies in most Japanese industries (Allouche, Amann, Jaussaud, and Kurashina, 2008).

Family Businesses: The Strengths

Overseas Chinese family businesses have some distinct characteristics as compared to other family businesses from other regions and ethnics. Nevertheless, by nature, a business owned and managed by a family has many advantages compared to a non-family business. These advantages can lead to better competitiveness, higher performance, and higher company value.

Independence of Actions

Since the shareholders of the company are family members, there is less pressure from the stock market to pursue only financial short-term goals. As a result, a family business can invest its money and concentrate its effort on pursuing the long-term objectives. Independence of action also relates to the decision-making process. Decisions and actions can be taken faster since the family holds full control of the business. While in a company such as a state-owned enterprise or a public limited company, many strategic decisions have to be approved by the shareholders, governments, and lawmakers before they can be implemented.

Strong Family Culture

Family culture becomes self-pride, which symbolizes stability, identity, motivation, strong commitment, and continuity in leadership. Family spirit creates values, norms, and an attitude in the company, while the values of family members express the creation of goals and objectives for employees. Businesses that survive and have good knowledge are those that have outstanding entrepreneurial spirit. Family members believe that their survival will depend on the survival of the business. If the business cannot survive, neither can they.

Long-Term Commitment

Long-term commitment is important to building the family and business reputation and increasing the company's brand value. Long-term commitment also makes many family businesses more cost-conscious and more conservative regarding funding decisions. As a result, they will be less likely to be trapped in a huge debt. Long-term orientation enables a company to focus on accomplishing its vision and mission. It will also motivate the family and employees to produce high-quality products and services.

Long-term commitment also serves as the foundation in attracting qualified employees, as well as promoting change and spirit of innovation. The absence of commitment will cast doubt among the company's stakeholders.

Speed and Flexibility

Centralized decision making, paternalistic leadership, and an emphasis on personal relationships give family businesses the ability to act more quickly and with more flexibility, which can lead to competitive advantage. Speed and flexibility are particularly needed when dealing with any crisis.

Speed is the most important element since a crisis requires an immediate action with no time to change the strategies and tactics in details. If not dealt with immediately, a crisis could have a destructive impact. Crisis requires flexibility as well. Usually a crisis will create side effects that cannot be clearly identified. Simple and flexible bureaucracy, supported by strong family ties based on high trust, enable a family business to make faster decisions to minimize the impact of the crisis, considering that every family member has a common interest in the business, which earns them a living and is a source of family pride.

In a business managed and controlled by family, family members can talk about business whenever and wherever they like. Ciputra, the founder of Ciputra Group, one of the leading property groups in Indonesia, once said that in a family business you can have meetings in the office, at the dining table, or even in your bedroom.

Learning Opportunities for Younger Generations

Since they were very young, the children of the founders have often been involved in helping with business activities, although they do it on a part-time basis and are not assigned significant tasks. For the children, family business provides opportunities to learn about the business and the importance of values such as hard work, sacrifice, respect, integrity, punctuality, trustworthiness, cooperation, and so on.

Opportunity to Work Together

Family business could be a place where family members, including siblings, can understand each other, build trust, and strengthen their relationship. It also can be a foundation to build a solid family team so that the family and the business can achieve their goals.

One example is Central Group from Thailand, which has survived more than two generations. The traditional practices introduced by Samrit Chirathivat, the son of the founder, Tiang Chirathivat, still continue today. This includes living and eating together. When eating together, the family usually talks about business issues. This tradition makes the bond and the relationship among Chirathivat family members very strong. They actively participate in the businesses. All businesses within the group are led by the family members.

Family Businesses: The Weaknesses

Despite all the strengths, the Chinese have a saying about family businesses: The first generation builds the company; the second generation grows the company; and the third generation destroys the company. Many family firms reject such a saying. They argue that it is only a myth, and that this saying must not be used as justification to stop striving for the company's and family's glory. Regardless, the fact is that many family businesses don't last for more than one generation. Many family businesses start to decline after the senior generation is no longer at the helm. This is because a family owned business has weaknesses that impede its progress.

Confusing Organization

Many family businesses lack clarity regarding rules and roles because there is no formal organizational structure. As a result, family members outside the company (for example, the wife of the founder, who doesn't hold any formal position) can also involve themselves in the company's activities, including giving orders and instructions to the employees. This undermines accountability within the family business.

Family Domination in the Business

Another weakness is the family dominance in the business, in which business logics are put behind family reasons. This is because family members cannot make a clear separation between family matters and business matters. As a result, bias in decision-making involving family is inevitable. This situation could create dissatisfaction and disappointment for the employees.

The absence of clear separation between family matters and business matters can create other negative consequences such as "milking the business," in which the influential family members use the revenue from the business for personal purposes. This certainly can weaken the company's financial resources, which are needed to spur growth and development.

Spoiled-Kid Syndrome

Spoiled-kid syndrome happens when the company recruits an incompetent family member just because he or she is a part of the family. This could create suspicion and jealousy among family members. Non-family members might also feel uncomfortable because they have to work with incompetent people. Recruiting an incompetent person will also undermine the business's competitiveness and performance.

Ownership and Management

Family ownership and management could create independence of action. Nevertheless, many family businesses are often too dependent on the owner, who acts as if he is capable of functioning in any role and handling all the problems. If something happens to the owner, the company could get into trouble.

Modernizing Overseas Chinese Family Businesses

The characteristics of a family business, with all strengths and weaknesses, are largely similar to Chinese values. The challenge is how the OCFB can minimize the weaknesses. This can be done by putting the values in the right context based on the principle "What is best for the business is the best for the family," although some values must not be compromised, such as integrity, honesty, hard work, and diligence. For example, harmony, solidarity, and seniority can be maintained as long as they bring benefits to the business, while cost-consciousness, a common feature in many OCFBs, should be balanced with the ability to take calculated risks so that potential investments can be made.

With such principles, family relationships and emotional bonding will become a source of strength so that the business can thrive. This in turn will strengthen the family and organizational culture. Unfortunately, many Chinese family businesses tend to be reactionary. They refuse to change, whereas business environments are changing very fast. Many reasons are cited, such as "respecting family tradition" and "maintaining family unity." However, such reasons are often mentioned to cover up the resistance to change.

Putting traditional values in the right context is only the beginning. Successful overseas Chinese family businesses adopt modern management practices. To do this, a family business must first build a solid organization. It must also focus on human resource development, promote open communication, focus on innovation, focus on customers, implement corporate governance, develop strategic planning, and move toward professionalism.

Building a Solid Organization

Every company, regardless of its ownership, always has to address seven organizational issues so that a solid organization can be built. Lack of attention to these issues could impede a company in achieving its goals, while serious attention regarding these issues would enable a company to understand its current position, which becomes the foundation for making any business decisions. These issues are leadership; strategic planning; customer and market focus; measurement, analysis, and knowledge management; human resources (HR) focus; process management; and business results.

Leadership. A company needs leadership that encourages its employees to strive to achieve its vision and goals. A leader has to have a clear, credible, and realistic vision and share it with all employees.

Strategic Planning. Planning encourages commitment from employees as part of the process. It also helps employees build common understanding and assumption regarding the environment in which a company operates.

Customer and Market Focus. Customer and market are the company's source of revenue, which enable a company to survive and grow. We are now seeing intense competition combined with rapid technological development. Customer behavior also changes fast. A company needs to address this trend so that it can thrive, survive, and stay competitive.

Measurement, Analysis, and Knowledge Management. Knowledge management comprises a range of strategies and practices used in a company to identify, create, distribute, and enable adoption of insights and experiences. Such insights and experiences comprise knowledge, either embodied in individuals or embedded in organizations as processes or practices.

HR Focus. HR focus is related to human resource management through skills and knowledge as the main contributor in achieving company vision, mission, and goals.

Process Management. Process management involves a set of activities regarding planning and monitoring of corporate performance. Process management is the application of skills, knowledge, techniques, and system to set, to measure, to control, and then to improve the process to meet the customer requirements.

Business Results. Business results are indicators measuring a company's financial and non-financial performance.

However, in a family business, merely addressing these issues, although important, is not enough. This is because in a family business, family relationships have to be taken into consideration. Therefore, alongside the seven issues mentioned previously, a family business should also focus its attention on seven other critical issues, which take family relationships into consideration. These are as follows:

Value Conflict

Value conflict happens mostly because of the differences between family and business values. Family values are built on emotion, life-long membership, and unchanging traditions, whereas business values tend to be task oriented and non-emotional. In business, reward is based on achievement and performance, not membership or relationship.

Succession

Succession is one of the most crucial issues in a family business, particularly when the younger generation starts to become involved in the business. Issues regarding succession include succession planning and potential conflicts among the younger generation.

Organizational Structure

Organizational structure relates to the placement of family members in the organization and the required competence should they want to join the business. If many of the family members were involved in the early stages of the business, there will be multiple leadership roles. But if the company is owned by only one person, usually there will be only one leader.

Compensation

Compensation relates to fairness for the family and non-family members and the amount of the compensation itself. Many family business owners experience difficulty in discussing this subject, particularly if the children of the founder also work for the business. As a result, compensation for the family members is often based on mixed principles of family and business.

Competence

Competence is also an important issue because of the limitations in human resource development and the resistance to change. One of the key success factors in a family business is its ability to manage the competence of the owners, managers, employees, and family members. To enhance its competence, a family business often changes corporate strategy, changes the corporate culture, changes the organizational structure, invests in resources to realize its vision, and replaces less competent people in strategic positions.

Revenue Distribution

Revenue distribution is related to the fairness of revenue distribution among family members. The main point is the percentage of the profit that should be used to grow and develop the firm and the percentage that should be distributed to the family members.

Alignment

Alignment between family and business objectives ensures that the operations of the business can run smoothly.

Focusing on Human Resource Development

In modern management practice, competent human resources are the most important asset. Therefore, it is important to provide continuous training and development to the employees, based on the company's needs.

Many Chinese family businesses are becoming more aware of this. Take the IOI Corporation Berhad, for example; one of the company's strengths is its professional, dedicated, and talented team of human capital. Various programs have been developed. For example, the Management Trainee program was developed with the purpose of grooming recent graduates to become the managers of tomorrow through proper exposure, mentoring, and career development. Ultimately, the objective of the program is to infuse the organization with renewal and a wealth of information and knowledge.

The importance of human resources is also acknowledged by Qian Hu, a Singapore-based ornamental fish service provider, with services ranging from the farming, importing, exporting, and distribution of ornamental fish, to their specialty of breeding Dragon Fish. It exports fish to more than 45 countries in the world with primary markets in Japan, China, Taiwan, the United Kingdom, Germany, and France, as well as to the rest of Europe and North Asia. Qian Hu has offices and outlets in three other countries: Malaysia, China, and Thailand. The history of Qian Hu began in the 1980s, when Yap Tik Huay, father of the current managing director, Kenny Yap, and Yap Tik Huay's brother, Yap Hey Cha, ran a pig farm. Yap Tik Huay and his brother were forced to convert their pig farm into a fish farm because at that time the Singapore government was closing all of the pig farms to make room for urban and residential developments. In 1993, Kenny Yap became the managing director, and under his leadership the management team introduced the performance-based reward system aimed at reducing the company's reliance on family members in the daily business operations. At the same time, Qian Hu's management also empowers key staff with greater job flexibility and responsibility.

Another example is Popular Holdings Limited (commonly called Popular). It is a Singapore-based company that publishes, distributes, and retails books for the local education market. It has subsidiaries in countries such as Canada, the People's Republic of China, Malaysia, Hong Kong, and Taiwan. Popular was established in 1924 by the late Chou Sing Chu, who migrated to Singapore from China. He is the father of the present chairman, Chou Cheng Ngok. Chou Cheng Ngok ensures his staff members constantly practice lifelong learning by undergoing a systematic developmental training curriculum that provides opportunities to develop their potential to the fullest.

Sinarmas Land, the subsidiary of Sinarmas, focuses on employee development through a clear career path in its business units, by strengthening the corporate culture and cooperation, and by striving to make Sinarmas Land an organization with excellent performance.

Career development for family members also has to be considered. The qualifications of family members should be evaluated and directed based on their talent and characteristics, to match them to the position. If a family member has a qualification, it needs to be decided whether he or she tends to have leadership characteristics or tends to have specialized professional qualifications. If he has leadership characteristics, we must look further to see whether he has the potential to be promoted to a higher managerial position. If he does, he could be appointed to key positions in the business. But if he doesn't, he can be given job enrichment.

However, if he tends to have a specialized professional qualification, he has to be developed as well. Is he able to deepen his skills and knowledge? If he is, he can be directed to be a certified professional. But if he is not, he also can be given job enrichment. This is the *dual career path* for family members, as shown in Figure 3.1.

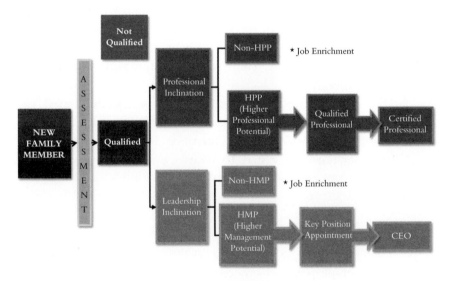

Figure 3.1 Dual career path for family members

Career development in a family firm aims at aligning strategy and the business plan. It also helps family members develop their talent, skills, and competence. Counseling, training and development, and career opportunities should be provided. Career development also aims at enhancing skills and knowledge.

Career development in a family business consists of six stages, namely orientation, identity building, maturity, stability, transition, and retirement, as shown in Table 3.1. In the orientation stage, family members try to find out whether they like their job. At this stage, they do not work for money and do not expect much. They also can be rotated from one department to another, which will give them complete understanding of the business. This stage can be done in the family firm; however, it can be more effective if the orientation is done in another company. Family members must be introduced to job knowledge, function knowledge, function responsibility, and so forth.

In the identity-building stage, family members start to be involved in the daily routine and join meetings so that they can give ideas, support, and suggestions. They must start to learn about interpersonal relationships problem management, conflict management, decision making, negotiation skills, industry knowledge, and leadership exposure.

In the maturity stage, after having experienced company exposure and working as a team, family members try to create systems and concepts. In this stage they need to develop skills such as political understanding, strategic planning, functional leadership, crisis management, and external relations. These skills come into play along with the greater responsibility.

In the stability stage, family members have already gained self-confidence, a tendency to expand, and a better living standard.

In the transition stage, family members become mentors to the younger generation. They start to focus on social activities, achieve quality of life, and are able to choose their successor.

Promoting Open Communication

Open communication has many benefits. It helps the company develop trust among employees and other people, including customers, investors, and suppliers. It also enhances cooperation and empowerment;

Table 3.1 Development Stages in a Family Business

No.	Stage & Age	Development Needs	Function
1	*Orientation* (21–25)	Job knowledge, functional knowledge, project responsibility, etc.	Tasting—like or dislike, atmosphere scanning (in & outside), work well without expecting much.
2	*Identity Building* (26–30)	Interpersonal relationships, problem management, conflict management, decision making, negotiation skills, industry knowledge, leadership exposure, etc.	"Setting in" routine management. Suggest, support, and refuse ideas. High remuneration awareness.
3	*Maturity* (31–40)	Political understanding, strategic planning, functional leadership, crisis management, and external relations.	Ability to work in a team. Concept creation & implementation. Need of good income.
4	*Stability* (41–45)	Visioning, risk taking, government influence, influence change, synergies or organization alignment, etc.	High self-confidence, tendency to expand, rising living standard.
5	*Transition* (56–65)	Counseling, retirement preparation, etc.	Mentor in charge. Involvement in social activities. Quality of life.
6	*Retirement* >66		Mentor at request. Estate planning. High spiritual life.

improves company and individual performance, quality of decision-making, and strategy execution; and promotes a positive environment. Open communication encourages employees to voluntarily spread positive opinion about the company to all external parties.

Focusing on Innovation and Technology

To compete in a fast-changing market, innovation is a must. Fortunately, many Chinese family businesses realize it. They do research and development (R&D) activities, set up R&D functions or departments, build an R&D center, and allocate funds for R&D. They also regularly launch new brands or rejuvenated ones. The story of Bertram Chemical— a Thai manufacturer and distributor of homeopathic, non-prescription herbal products—can prove this. The company was founded by Boonchua Eiampikul, who immigrated to Thailand from Shanton in Southeast China when he was a young boy. His involvement in herbal products started soon after he met Tang Leng Yong, a practitioner in traditional Chinese medicine who immigrated to Thailand at the same time and since then had become a close friend of Boonchua Eiampikul's parents. He passed on his knowledge about Chinese traditional medicine to Boonchua.

Boonchua began producing a medicinal herbal oil called Siang Pure Oil, which he sold in small quantities within the Chinese community in Bangkok. Siang Pure Oil is an herbal oil whose mixture is based upon a secret traditional formula passed on over generations among practitioners of traditional Chinese medicine in the Shantou region.

Boonchua set up The Chakrintr Ltd. Partnership in 1963. He did this to increase the presence of Siang Pure Oil in the market because more people wanted to buy it. This company started from humble beginnings since there were only two people involved: Boonchua himself as CEO and another person whose job was to market the product. Siang Pure Oil was marketed across Thailand. The company was later named Bertram Chemical Works Ltd. as more and more people acknowledged Siang Pure Oil's high quality. In 1982, Boonchua again changed the company's name. This time, he named the company Bertram Chemical Co., the same year his daughter joined the business.

However, many younger customers were not interested in Siang Pure Oil since they thought that it was a product for older persons, whereas the number of young people in Thailand, as well as in neighboring countries, was larger and growing faster. Facing such a situation, a new strategy was set up to make Siang Pure Oil more attractive to young people. A new herbal oil called Siang Pure Oil Formula II was launched. In this new product, although the recipe was not changed, the old mixture had been reformulated.

Today, the number of products offered by Bertram Chemical has increased. These include Siang Pure Inhaler, Peppermint Field Gel,

Peppermint Field Balm Stick, and See Chuan Oil. Nevertheless, Siang Pure Oil is still the largest contributor. Bertram Chemical still has to buy the raw material needed for the products from China. The quality of the product has to be maintained. To support the production process, Bertram Chemical uses modern manufacturing technology, applies quality control, and sets up R&D.

Innovation is not only limited to the products, but must also include marketing activities. Again, many OCFBs are familiar with this. In fact, they have done this in their early years, although the innovation seemed simple.

One example is Sinar Sosro. Sosro is the pioneer of packaged ready-to-drink tea in Indonesia. The name Sosro is taken from the name of the founding family, Sosrodjojo. In 1940, the Sosrodjojo family started their business in a small city in Central Java called Slawi. At the time, the product sold was dried tea with the brand of "Teh Cap Botol" and was distributed only around Central Java.

The journey to introduce the Teh Cap Botol product was started by doing Cicip Rasa (product tasting) promotions at several markets in Jakarta. The promotion was conducted by entering the markets and brewing the Teh Cap Botol tea product on the spot. When the tea was ready, it was distributed to people on site. This promotion was not too successful as the distributed tea was too hot to drink and the brewing process took too long, making those waiting to taste it impatient.

The next method they used was brewing the tea elsewhere, then carrying the already-brewed tea in big pans to the markets using open trucks. Again, this was unsuccessful because some of the tea spilled on the way to the market, mostly due to the badly pockmarked roads in Jakarta at the time.

Then, an idea sprang up to carry the brewed tea in cleaned bottles. It turned out that this method was quite interesting for the customers because it was practical and the tea was brewed and ready to consume. In 1969, the idea to sell ready-to-drink tea in a bottle was formulated, and in 1970, a bottled tea plant of PT Sinar Sosro was established, the first-ever bottled ready-to-drink tea plant in Indonesia and in the world.

Sosro has been run by three Sosrodjojo generations. The first generation is Sosrodjojo (deceased), the Sosro group founder. The second generation includes Soemarsono Sosrodjojo (deceased), Soegiharto Sosrodjojo, Soetjipto Sosrodjojo, and Surjanto Sosrodjojo. And since early 1990, the business has been managed by the grandchildren of Sosrodjojo (the third generation). The beverage business development has since then been done by two companies, namely Sinar Sosro and Gunung Slamat. Sinar Sosro is a company that produces packaged ready-to-drink tea.

The story of Krating Daeng in Thailand is another example. Krating Daeng is a sweetened, noncarbonated energy drink developed by Chaleo Yoovidhya. The drink is mostly sold in Asia but can be found in Austria, Sweden, Denmark, Australia, Canada, New Zealand, and the United States. Mr. Chaleo took the name from the gaur, a large wild bovine of Southeast Asia. Krating Daeng became the basis for the creation of the best-selling energy drink in the world, Red Bull. The recipe is based on Bacchus-F of South Korea and Lipovitan of Japan, earlier energy drinks that were introduced to Thailand. It contains water, cane sugar, caffeine, taurine, inositol, and B-vitamins.

Krating Daeng sales soared across Asia in the 1970s and 1980s, especially among truck drivers, construction workers, and farmers. The most important factor behind its rapid rise was Chaleo's unconventional marketing, which saw him ignore Bangkok, home to wealthier consumers. He positioned Red Bull to appeal to laborers and blue-collar workers: a low-cost product advertised heavily with popular giveaways that appealed to truck drivers, construction workers, and shift workers. According to one of his sons, Saravuth, his father stressed brand building, a marketing strategy that had not been widely employed up to that time. Truck drivers would drink it to stay awake during the long, late-night drive. The working-class image was boosted by sponsorship of Thai boxing matches, where the logo of two red bulls charging each other was often on display. The Thai product was transformed into a global brand by Dietrich Mateschitz, an Austrian entrepreneur. Mateschitz was international marketing director for Blendax, a German toothpaste company, when he visited Thailand in 1982 and discovered that Krating Daeng helped to cure his jet lag. He cooperated with Chaleo's T.C. Pharmaceuticals, adapted the formula and composition with no animal ingredients, and to western tastes. Red Bull was launched in 1987.

Chaleo himself was born into a poor Thai Chinese immigrant family that raised ducks and traded fruit in Phichit. With little formal education, he worked for his parents and then moved to Bangkok to help his brother run his chemist's shop. He learned much about importing and distribution, which would help him later. He became an antibiotics salesman before quitting to set up his own small pharmaceutical company, T.C. Pharmaceuticals, in the early 1960s. Partnership with Dietrich Mateschitz was established in 1984. In 1987, the two launched an export version labeled "Red Bull," for which Chaleo provided the formula and Mateschitz the marketing. Each put up US$500,000, for 49 percent of the Red Bull energy drink franchise, with Chaleo's son, Chalerm, owning the remaining. Chaleo continued to own T.C. Pharmaceuticals, which manufactured other energy drinks in Thailand, and was part owner of Piyavate Hospital, a private hospital in Thailand. Chaleo died in Bangkok on March 17, 2012. *Forbes* magazine ranked Chaleo as the world's 205th richest person. He was one of five billionaires from Thailand to appear on *Forbes'* 2012 list of the World's Billionaires.

In addition to energy drinks, Chaleo businesses include a hospital chain, a winery in Thailand, and two international soccer teams, namely the New York Red Bulls and Red Bulls Salzburg in Austria.

Chalerm Yoovidhya runs the flagship company as well as his wine business, Siam Winery. He co-owns a Ferrari dealership and supports the Red Bull racing team.

Alongside innovation, science and technology is also used by many Chinese family businesses to improve efficiency and increase production. One example is IOI Corporation Berhad, one of the most efficient palm oil producers (Mason, 2011). This strength stems from IOI's belief that the most efficient business model can be a very effective environmental model. Based on this model, IOI strategizes to maximize outputs from their plantations and factories while minimizing the inputs required using an efficient and effective plantation management program. The efficient use of land translates into lower fertilizer, pesticide, and energy usage as well as benefits for the environment. The end result is a dramatically reduced demand for land required to produce the volumes demanded by the market.

In its annual reports, IOI claims that its superior performance in terms of oil yield and production cost per hectare compared to the industry's average is partly attributable to its advances in agronomy sciences, which are spearheaded by its two centers of excellence, IOI Research Centre and Tissue Culture Center.

Developing Strategic Planning in a Family Business

The future is marked by a fast-changing environment. To anticipate the change, it's important for a company to develop a strategic plan, a common practice in a modern organization and company.

In strategic planning, an organization defines its strategy and makes decisions regarding resource allocation to implement the strategy. The company must predict the future, supported by adequate data and thorough analysis. For the family, strategic planning will drive commitment, develop business knowledge, and serve as a means for younger generations to learn about the business. The strategic planning process will help family members and non-family employees reach common understanding regarding the surrounding environment. The strategic planning will also help the family reveal the soundness of the business. One thing that needs to be examined is how much money the family has reinvested for business purposes and how much money has been distributed to the family members.

Unfortunately, many family businesses are still reluctant to develop strategic planning since they are not used to it. In many family businesses where the founder still rejects any help from outside the family, as we find in many Chinese family businesses, strategic planning will make them reveal confidential data, weak communication management practices, past mistakes, and family problems. They also think that strategic planning will limit their flexibility. Strategic planning processes also require founders to share the decision-making process and submit financial reports.

In a company, strategic planning can be divided into three steps. First is aligning organizational interest with stakeholder interest. A stakeholder is a person, group, organization, or system that affects or can be affected by an organization's actions—such as customers, employees, shareholders, suppliers, the community, and the government. Each company has different stakeholders, so a company has to be able to identify them. Second is developing organizational strategy, starting with formulating the vision and mission. Next, the company must set its strategic objectives. Strategic objectives have to be realistic, challenging, measurable, consistent, and clear. Therefore, a company must understand its strengths and weaknesses, opportunities, and threats from the outside. In other words, a company must conduct a *SWOT* (Strengths, Weaknesses, Opportunities, and Threats) analysis.

A company must also evaluate its portfolio. After the strategic objectives are set, the company can develop a strategy—that is, how strategic objectives can be accomplished. The company should also develop *critical success factors*, elements that are necessary for a company to ensure the strategy can work according to plan. Third is to develop a business plan, that is, developing functional strategies for each department. In developing a business plan, a company must consider risk management, in which events that can have a negative effect are identified, measured, and controlled. As part of functional strategy development, the company must set achievement targets to motivate the employees and to focus programs and activities. Fourth is implementing the plan. The implementation should be evaluated to find out whether it works according to plan.

In implementing strategic planning, a company must develop the right organizational structure. Then, it must develop the organizational culture, that is, values guiding employees when performing their duties and behavior in the company. These values will determine whether an employee does the right thing, or whether certain values are encouraged. Leadership also plays an important role. A company needs leaders who can help employees realize their potential. Weak leadership makes strategy implementation fail. In family businesses, weak leadership seldom occurs while the first generation is still at the helm. Chinese family businesses should be able to take advantage of this situation to develop comprehensive and credible strategic planning.

However, in a family firm, strategic planning must take the family into consideration. The starting point for the strategic planning process is the family. The family must develop commitments for the business and a plan to keep them. The commitments include the readiness to sacrifice short-term financial profit for long-term investment, spending time to run the business, working together as a team, and willingness to hand over control to the senior generation.

Moving toward Professionalism

Professionalism means the methods, character, and status of a professional. A professional is someone who has skills and knowledge in a certain field; performs high-quality work; and has a high standard of professional ethics, behavior, and work activities. A family business needs professionals with such characteristics, and they often have to be recruited from outside the family because the family does not have adequate skills and knowledge. Professionals can also help the family members evaluate business ideas and strategies and give them a more objective view.

Professionalism will help a family firm move toward modernity. Professionalism is required in leadership, information gathering, knowledge management, image building, accountability, and human resource competence.

In 1995, Central Group switched its orientation from focusing mainly on the family goal to focusing more on the business goal. As Suthichart Chirathiwat said, "This was due to the fact that Samrit was the head of the family, while all the family members supported him in business. Therefore, the business at that time was very much family oriented. After he passed away, the family felt the pressure to move away from family oriented business to professional business. The management role of the family council was reduced, while the board of directors was established."

Many successful overseas Chinese family firms have recruited professionals to the business. Eu Yan Sang is one example. It is a company that specializes in traditional Chinese medicine. It currently runs more than 160 retail outlets in Hong Kong, Macau, China, Malaysia, and Singapore, plus two factories in Hong Kong and Malaysia. The group also operates 21 TCM clinics in Malaysia and Singapore and two integrative medical centers in Hong Kong. The company headquarters are in Singapore. Eu Yan Sang was founded in 1879 in Gopeng, Perak, Malaysia, by Eu Kong Pai, better known as Eu Kong. Today, the company is led by the fourth generation of Eu Kong's family and more professionals are recruited for senior management positions.

CP, Thailand is another example. CP does not bring in family members to manage existing business, but it recruits outside professionals. Dhanin Chearavanont, the current CEO, as quoted by Vorabandhit (2004), said, "CP Group doesn't need to place family members into already successful businesses. These businesses are successful because good managers are there and they should be encouraged to pursue the good work they are doing. For the able family members, we can afford to give them the resources to build new businesses. This way, they can build the name for themselves and CP can extend its empire."

Andrew Tan from Alliance Global Group, Philippines, said that his companies were publicly listed. All are professionally managed. He always has to keep in mind that they are not running a family business anymore. He doesn't force his children to work for him. Having said that, one of his children is a middle manager; another is a junior manager. They report to their senior managers, not to him.

Professionalism needs support from both family members and non-family employees. Both sides must adjust their attitudes and behavior and work together harmoniously. Family members must give non-family professionals more authority to make important decisions.

Chapter 4

Anatomy of Conflict Management

History has shown us that many family businesses can last for many generations. For example, in Indonesia, many family businesses have lasted for almost a century. Their leaders possess the strong entrepreneurial spirit that makes them resilient and able to cope with many challenges. Take the herb industry, for example. Many herb companies in Indonesia started their business from a small home industry. At the beginning, they practiced traditional management and used traditional technology. However, as time went by, they were able to combine the ancient philosophy of herbs and medicine with modern science and technology. In anticipating changes in consumer preference, they develop research-based products, supported with money, facility, and professional manpower. Many of these herb companies are owned by Indonesian Chinese.

The existence of family businesses is often threatened by internal instead of external factors, such as bitter family conflict. Bitter family conflict causes disruption to the company's activities, decreasing performance and causing lower employee morale, physical and mental fatigue, divided attention, and a loss in synergy.

The Story of Nyonya Meneer

Conflict at Nyonya Meneer, one of the biggest herb companies in Indonesia, is widely known. Charles Saerang, the current president director and a third-generation Nyonya Meneer family member, has to deal with three conflicts.

Nyonya Meneer started her herb business to support her family after her husband passed away. The company expanded rapidly and Nyonya Meneer involved her children to help run the company. She passed away in 1978 at the age of 83.

Nyonya Meneer had five children, Nonie, Hans Ramana, Lucie, Marie, and Hans Pangemanan. The three conflicts began soon after the passing of the company's founder, Nynya Meneer. Two years earlier, Hans Ramana, Charles's father, who was expected to take over the business, died of cancer. Charles, who had just come back to Indonesia after finishing his studies abroad, and without any experience in managing the family business, had to deal with his uncle and aunt, who had children older than he. However, his uncle and aunt still trusted him, and after he asked to represent his father's family and to be given a chance, he began handling the marketing department.

Thanks to his marketing programs, by the mid-1980s Nyonya Meneer's market share, sales, and profits were at record highs. However, not all members of the family were happy. The costs of running advertising campaigns drew heavy criticism from some parts of the family. During this period two clear sides emerged. Hans Pangemanan as president director and Nonie Saerang as commissioner approved Charles's marketing campaigns, while Marie and Lucie as the other commissioners disapproved the expenditure and wanted a more active role in the management of the company. Charles and Hans Pangemanan secretly met with Sudomo, the Minister of Manpower at that time, and told him of the management problems in the company and that the only way to fix them would be if he would step in. Sudomo agreed to mediate with the shareholders.

After months of mediation, a compromise was reached. Hans Pangemanan would stay as president director, and Marie's son, Fitzimons Kalalo, would be appointed his deputy. Unfortunately, Hans and Fitzimons Kalalo could not agree on anything and the conflict between the two groups deepened. Decisions were made by both directors that contradicted each other, and thousands of the company's employees were forced to choose a side. On January 1985, a fight broke out between an employee loyal to Fitzimons and the head of Security, who was loyal to Hans. The long and bitter conflict had seriously affected the company's production, and 1,300 employees were laid off. On November 28, 1985, Sudomo organized a mediation meeting between the two groups in Jakarta. The differences in management were too great and the only solution was for one party to buy out the other party. Marie and Lucie agreed to sell their 40 percent block of shares to Hans, Nonie, and Charles. According to the agreement at that time, Hans would stay on as the company's president director, Charles as the marketing director, and Nonie as commissioner.

As the president director since 1985, Hans led the company in a manner similar to his mother. This included living in Semarang, developing strong ties with all the workers, and keeping control of every aspect of the company. He preferred stability to growth, and this led to constant differences of opinion with his nephew. Charles was convinced that in order for the company to thrive in the new millennium they would have to have a reorganization of the management structure.

During the annual shareholders meeting in December 1989, Charles was appointed president director of Nyonya Meneer. For the next ten months, Charles completely restructured and streamlined the executive management and human resources department management. Job descriptions were made transparent. Hans informed Charles that his appointment as president director the previous December was illegal and Hans would resume operational control of the company.

In October 1990, Hans brought evidence that there was a procedural error in the signing of the president director appointment. He claimed that as Gwyneth, Charles's sister, had taken Australian citizenship, she was forbidden to vote. Charles knew it didn't matter if one of the commissioners was a foreign national or not. Angrily, he called for an extraordinary meeting of the shareholders to resolve this issue once and for all. The meeting was held in Jakarta on December 14, 1990. Both sides were unwilling to compromise and Charles decided to leave the meeting. After an hour, all sides reconvened in the conference room. Nonie declared that all of Hans's duties would be immediately suspended and temporarily assigned to the president commissioner. The initial reason for Hans' suspension was that he failed to report the company's financial statement to the Board of Commissioners during his entire tenure as president director from 1984 to 1989. Hans rejected the decision and threatened to tell the story of the turmoil at Nyonya Meneer. Because of the deadlock, the meeting would reconvene one month later to decide Hans's fate.

On January 12, 1991, the meeting was reassembled in the Sahid Jaya Hotel in Jakarta. The main reason for this meeting would be for Hans to explain why he did not report any financial statements during his tenure, but Hans refused to attend. He claimed that on the invitation he was listed as a shareholder and not as the suspended president director.

The remaining shareholders decided that this had gone far enough. They had shown goodwill giving Hans a chance to defend himself and were rebuffed. They decided unanimously that Hans Pangemanan was dismissed as president director effective December 14, 1990. Charles was appointed as the new president director; Nonie resigned from the board of commissioners. Vera Saerang, Charles's mother, and Nonie's husband, Oka, would be appointed the new commissioners.

As expected, Hans rejected this decision. He argued that he was not given the opportunity to defend himself. Three days after the vote to dismiss him, he sued the six shareholders (his sister, his sister-in-law, and four nephews) in Semarang Court on January 15, 1991. He demanded the January 12, 1991, meeting be declared illegal, confiscation of all properties and land owned by the company, and damages in the amount of 5 billion rupiahs (about US$2.5 million at the time).

While the court was processing these accusations, Nyonya Meneer continued to have two president directors, and neither of them would give up their positions. Hans refused to vacate the office of the president director, seized corporate and shareholder documents, and continued to use letterhead and sign agreements as president director. Hans's sons, Finance Director Power Pangemanan and the head of the Delivery Bureau, Linky Pangemanan, refused to follow any instructions issued by Charles and claimed loyalty to their father as president director. Charles tried to reclaim his position as president director by trying to win support from the mayor of Semarang and the chief justice of Semarang's civil court.

Worrying about the potential devastating impact this conflict could have on the company's employees, the mayor of Semarang at the time, Soetrisno Soeharto, initiated a meeting of both parties in his official residence. Five agreements were made during that meeting. First, the president director's office would be left vacant until there was a decision from the court. Second, the president director's office would be locked and guarded by the police. Third, Hans and Charles would temporarily accept the position of vice president. Fourth, their job descriptions would be determined later in the next meeting. And fifth, the mayor would explain the current situation to all of the company's employees.

On August 15, 1991, the judge handed down the verdict. The case of Hans was considered legally weak and was thrown out. Charles was to resume his role as president director effective immediately. Hans immediately filed an appeal with the high court of Central Java. On December 22, 1991, the high court of Central Java upheld the lower court decision. Not giving up, Hans filed an appeal with the Supreme Court and on August 31, 1993, the Supreme Court announced they would not hear the appeal and upheld both previous verdicts. The battle for leadership of Nyonya Meneer was officially over.

Hans sold his shares to Charles and Nonie. The mediation was led by Lucie's son, John. The parties agreed on a price in less than three months. The share transfer agreement was signed on June 1, 1994. With this agreement, Nyonya Meneer was now legally owned by two of the founder's heirs: her eldest daughter Nonie and her grandson Charles.

Nonie and her husband, Oka, had six children but only three, Peter, Paul, and Tony, had any involvement in the company. From Charles's side, his mother Vera, and his sisters, Gwyneth and Fiona, were commissioners. Each side owned 50 percent of the company. In the beginning, both sides worked together to manage and build the company. The problem started when Charles and his mother granted some shares to parties outside of the family. While not against the company's article of associations, Tony objected to this transfer. In the shareholder meeting on August 12, 1995, a resolution nominating Charles and Gwyneth as directors and Vera, Oka, and Fiona as commissioners was passed. Tony filed a lawsuit against Charles in November 1995 in Semarang. Tony's claim was that Charles had granted shares to an external party, and he felt that only members of the family should hold them. He also wanted Charles to resign as president director. The judge dismissed the case. Like his uncle Hans, Tony appealed to the high court as well as to the Supreme Court but each time the appeal was dismissed.

After Tony's case was rejected, Nonie filed suit in the District Court of Central Jakarta with the same case. On June 18, 1997, the court bizarrely reversed its previous decision. In the preliminary decision, the court declared the previous board appointment not in line with the shareholders' agreement. The judge also pronounced Paul, Tony's brother, to replace Charles as president director.

Charles was stunned. In celebration of the promotion, on June 21, 1997, Paul placed advertisements in major newspapers announcing Charles was no longer president director of Nyonya Meneer and reminded all business parties not to engage in any transactions with him. Paul also mentioned that Lindawaty Suryadinata, Charles's wife, was appointed to the Board of Commissioners, causing speculation that there were marital troubles between Charles and Lindawaty.

Charles felt that his reputation was tarnished and that he was slandered in public, and he reported the advertisement to the district police of Central Java. Charles's lawyer claimed that what Paul did was criminal. Furthermore, by announcing that Charles's wife was appointed to the Board of Commissioners (without her knowledge or approval), Paul himself violated the company's article of associations as a change in directors can be approved only in a shareholders meeting.

On July 3, 1997, Paul was summoned to the district police headquarters of Central Java to provide testimony. Paul admitted that he had made a mistake in making the announcement. He was found guilty and spent one week in prison. Newspapers around the country published stories of Paul's imprisonment and the experience changed him forever. Soon after his release, Nonie announced that she had agreed to sell her shares to Charles. For the first time since the death of the founder, all shares were held by one family. There were three share-holders: Charles, Vera, and Gwyneth.

The Story of Yeo Hiap Seng (YHS)

The story of YHS is summarized from the book titled *Wealth Doesn't Last 3 Generations: How Family Businesses Can Maintain Prosperity*, by Jean Lee and Hong Li (2008).

Yeo Hiap Seng Limited (YHS) is an investment holding company as well as a drink manufacturer in Singapore and Malaysia. It is a multi-national corporation that has offices and market presence in the United States, Europe, Australia, New Zealand, Maldives, Mauritius, Mongolia, the Pacific Islands, China, Hong Kong, Cambodia, Myanmar, Laos, Vietnam, and Japan. It produces its own Asian drinks and has the license from Pepsico to produce Pepsi, 7-Up, Mountain Dew, Mirinda, and Mug Root Beer. In addition, Yeo's also exclusively manages other international brands such as Red Bull, Gatorade, Evian, Volvic, Uni-President, Allswell, Hain Celestial, and Erika Dairies. The company has operations in over 60 countries, including Thailand, China, Singapore, Malaysia, and the United States, and franchises in Indonesia and Mauritius.

Established in 1901 in Zhangzhou, Fujian Province, by Yeo Keng Lian (Renliu), YHS traded mainly in the sauce industry. Mr. Yeo had eight children, five boys and three girls. In 1935, Yeo Keng Lian, because of poor health, handed over his factory to his eldest son, Yeo Thian In, who was only 22 years of age at that time. Mr. Yeo made the announcement at the celebration of his 60th birthday.

Thian In first worked as a traveling salesman, selling products manufactured in his sauce factory. His hard work eventually paid off. The sauce factory enjoyed a booming business. Soon, YHS products flooded the market in Zhangzhou. Thian In sent his younger brothers and sisters to colleges in inland China and even to Japan.

Having suffered tremendously from the political turbulence of China at that time, the Yeo brothers decided to leave their hometown and settle down in Singapore. The reason for moving to Singapore was its cultural background and climate. And since most of the Chinese in Singapore came from Fujian, they could communicate with each other freely. The hot weather in Singapore also made it easier for soybeans to ferment. The low price of salt was another favorable condition to develop the business of sauce making. In February 1937, Thian In, together with his wife and children, moved to Singapore. In autumn of the same year, the two younger brothers, Thian Kiew and Thian Seng, arrived in the city. They settled down and soon rented a plot of land at Outram Road to build the YHS sauce factory in Singapore.

After their college education, Thian In's brothers and sisters joined the family enterprise. YHS started from scratch, and over the a period of time witnessed rapid growth in the business. The brothers modernized their food factory through automation, gaining wide recognition from the public. At the same time, the brothers diversified their business by employing the bottled soymilk patent invented by their nephew, Chen Chee De. With their success in Singapore, they set out to conquer the market in Malaysia, thus starting the YHS business venture abroad. As the business grew, the family also expanded. In 1956, the five brothers signed an agreement dividing the estate of YHS into seven parts, shared among the five brothers, the eldest grandson, Chee Ming, and Chee Kiat. The five brothers are Thian In, Thian Kiew, Thian Seng, Thian Hwa, and Thian Soo.

As stated in the agreement, Thian In was recommended to be the permanent chairman and general manager, Thian Soo the vice chairman, and Chee Kiat the permanent finance director. It was also agreed that the number of directors should be five, but with the provision to add two more in the future. In addition, it was also agreed that three of Thian In's offspring and one each of Thian Soo's, Thian Kiew's, and Thian Hwa's offspring should be directors (by succession). The offspring of Thian In and Thian Soo, if they are interested in the work of the factory, should be given priority in management positions. Offspring of the Yeo families who have no interest in the work of the factory may find other jobs, but they should never borrow the name of YHS or do anything detrimental to the company. In the agreement, it was also prescribed that the board of directors should draw a certain portion of the company's earnings to set up a scholarship, providing the Yeo offspring with financial assistance for their college education. Upon their graduation, those offspring funded by the company's scholarship should be encouraged to work in the company. If they should choose not to work in the company, they would be required to contribute 20 percent of their income to the company for the first four years of employment. It was a well-crafted agreement, setting up guidelines for the division of family property, assignment of position to family members, and cultivation and education of offspring, which indeed greatly promoted the future development of YHS.

The 1960s witnessed a golden period for YHS. As a pioneer of local companies in Singapore that ventured abroad, YHS established a business network covering Malaysia, Hong Kong, and even Europe. Plans for a public listing were made in 1968. In order to prevent the company from falling into the hands of others, the family members decided to establish a holding company jointly controlled by the family. In 1969, YHS was listed and YHS Holding Company held 49 percent of shares of the listed YHS, reinforcing YHS's strength in the industry. The company took the lead in the beverage and canned-food market when it was given exclusive dealership in the region by Pepsi. In 1971, YHS built a factory in Malaysia. Three years later, YHS (Malaysia) Ltd. was established and in 1975 listed on the Malaysia Stock Exchange. The 1980s was a pivotal period for YHS, during which the company carried on a series of reforms and innovations in strategy, product renovation, operation management, and organizational structure. By so doing, the listed company performed well and enjoyed a leading role in the beverage market.

YHS invested in a lot of scientific research to promote the variety and packaging of beverages. The company developed many popular Asian-style products such as iced tea, sugarcane juice, and blended juice. In addition to its agreement on bottling and distribution with Pepsi, YHS also reached an agreement with Beecham (Production) Singapore Co. Ltd. to package and distribute Ribena to retail stores through the direct sales network of YHS. In 1985, YHS got in touch with Gatorade, a famous American brand, and was licensed the right to produce and distribute 7-Up, its beverage product. Focusing on the food and beverage market, YHS became a leader in the market of non-carbonated soft-drinks in Singapore. It was also one of the leaders in the condiments and canned-food market.

To enhance the growth of products and market, the company signed a software contract for US$1.6 million, aimed at fostering a computer-assisted management environment for manufacturing. In addition, the company introduced a bottling production line with a production capability of 1,000 bottles per minute, making it the fastest production speed in Southeast Asia. As early as the 1970s, YHS introduced packaging technology with plastic bottles for Pepsi and Minolta products, becoming the first in Asia to bottle soft-drinks with pull-tab cans.

In the 1990s, with the third generation of the Yeo family at its helm, problems emerged in YHS. Family members were divided on investment and management decisions. Although decisions in the company had always been made by a majority vote, it became increasingly difficult for family members to come to a consensus. The relationships among family members became increasingly complicated, which adversely affected the management of the company. When the third generation of the Yeo family was at the helm of YHS, Alan Yeo, a son of the eldest brother, Thian In, took the position of chairman and president of YHS Ltd. Some family members were asked to relinquish and resign from their senior and managerial positions in the company, resulting in the breakdown of relationships among family members and a loss of trust and affection that they had cherished since the founding of the company. In 1992, Thian Seng and three other family members were asked to resign. Devastated, Thian Seng's family decided to sell their shares and rights issue of the holding company. At the same time, Yeo Chee Wei, the son of Thian Kiew, having been removed from his position as executive director, also planned to sell his shares of the company. It was prescribed in the founding charter of the holding company that any withdrawal of shares of the holding company by any family member must be under the consent of other shareholders. Therefore, the holding company made plans to sell the shares at a higher price to the Keppel Group, a company that was interested in acquiring shares of YHS. Part of the fund was to be reserved for the company's use. However, when it was discovered that the prospective buyer was a third party, the families changed their mind. In the hope of upholding the position of the family as a whole in the holding company, they decided to sell only their shares but not the rights issue, thus bankrupting the share-selling program. The conflict intensified when Alan Yeo, having negotiated with the Keppel Group, communicated with the other families, except two, on the sale price. The management style of Alan Yeo was considered autocratic by other family members, as he made decisions without consulting other directors. On one occasion, he tried to purchase 140,000 shares (4.32 percent) for his son, Timothy Yeo, in the hope of obtaining more than a 50 percent share ownership for absolute control. Alan Yeo's move greatly disappointed other family members, who felt betrayed by his actions, and the rift between them deepened.

On April 22, 1994, Wing Tai Holding Ltd., a company dealing in real estate and garment manufacturing, proposed to purchase a huge number of ordinary shares of YHS through Citicorp Investment Bank (Singapore). The sum of the shares accounted for 25.5 to 40 percent of the total issued shares of YHS. Alan Yeo, one of the controlling shareholders of YHS, delivered an announcement in his personal capacity through Citicorp to support the purchase of YHS by Wing Tai Holdings.

However, other members of the family, who jointly held 53 percent of the total shares, did not agree with the purchase. Instead, they demanded a buy-back of the 47 percent of YHS shares owned by the three family members, including Alan Yeo's. In addition, they asked Alan Yeo, chairman of the company, to resign. The opposing side held the opinion that the listed YHS Ltd. should be run by professional managers instead of YHS Holdings. Alan Yeo, in his personal capacity, announced that the three families in support of the purchase would not sell their shares to the other shareholders.

It was the right of shareholders, not others, to decide if he stayed or resigned. In his opinion, the other six families did not share a common understanding and point of view. Under such conditions, the holding company should be dissolved instead of being retained. Only by so doing could each family hold direct shares of YHS and avoid unnecessary dispute in the future. A shareholders' meeting was held the following day and a decision was made to deny the purchase option as proposed by Wing Tai.

On July 1, 1994, the high court adjudicated YHS Holding Company Private Limited to be dissolved. Based on the understanding that the relationship of trust and dependence among the family members no longer existed, the verdict recognized that decision making by consensus among shareholders in the holding company was impossible. If business decisions were made by vote, it meant that the pattern of a holding company similar to a partnership ended and a new structure was born. Under such circumstances, the dissolution of the holding company was inevitable.

After the dissolution of YHS Holdings, the shares of YHS Ltd. owned by members of the Yeo family were gradually dispersed. Major changes also took place at the management level of YHS Ltd. Among the many family members who left YHS, Alan Yeo, on February 6, 1995, resigned from the board and from all of the positions in the subsidiary companies and allied companies.

Currently, Yeo Hiap Seng Limited is the subsidiary of Far East Organization, the largest private property developer in Singapore, founded by Singaporean billionaire Ng Teng Fong in the 1960s.

The Origins of Conflicts in Overseas Chinese Family Businesses

Conflict in a family business can be defined as a situation in the workplace in which two or more persons or groups in the family have opposing ideas, views, arguments, perceptions, and opinions so that they blame each other. This situation could have negative effects on the business. The origins of conflicts within family businesses vary. We will discuss them here.

Differences Regarding Business Interest and Family Interest

A family business is a combination of two institutions, namely family and business. Each institution has opposing values and goals (Figure 4.1). A family tends to be inward looking and decisions are made mostly based on emotional consideration, and family members accept them almost unconditionally. Sharing among family members is common; they often help and encourage each other. The membership in a family is limitless and almost impossible to be ceased. Family values are deeply embedded and also tend to resist change.

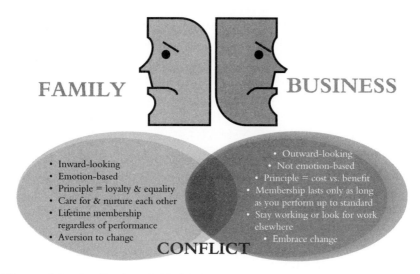

Figure 4.1 Conflict in a family business

On the contrary, a business is more outward looking. The ties between employees and managers are based on the tasks and commitment so that the emotional bond might not exist. Good performance will be rewarded. Those who fail to meet expectations will be terminated or asked to leave the business. While in a family there is resistance to change, in business change, is always necessary so that the company can survive and thrive.

Such opposing values often affect the electiveness of human resource management in the family business. Human resource management consists of policies such as recruitment and selection, compensation, performance evaluation, career development, and training and skill development. However, in a family business, emotional bonds often affect such policies.

In recruitment and selection, family members often feel that they have a right to be part of the business. They ask for a job in the business without considering their competence, and argue that family members should help each other unconditionally. However, a company, if it wants to progress, it should recruit only qualified individuals. Such individuals often have to be hired from outside the family business. Too many unqualified individuals will have a negative impact on business performance.

Compensation for family members is often based on the criteria and principles that mix the family and business interests. The situation gets worse when compensation received is not equal to the required contribution, and feelings of unfairness will emerge. This in turn will undermine trust, and low trust can have a negative impact on company climate, work satisfaction, motivation, and performance.

Regarding performance evaluation, family businesses often find it difficult to evaluate family members working in the company. If leaders or founders of a family business evaluate performance, bias might be difficult to avoid. The situation might be even worse if other employees cover up the incompetence of family members in order to keep their job safe.

Leaders of family businesses also often find it hard to decide on training and development for family members, especially regarding the separation between individual interest and business development. From the family point of view, training for family members should focus on "what is in the best interest of the individual family member" regardless of the business need. But from the company's point of view, training should emphasize the individual's improvement in learned skills, while helping to achieve the company's goal and objectives. Inability to align the individual interest and business needs regarding training and development will result in a waste of resources, while the company's performance will not improve.

Poor human resources management in many family businesses creates negative impacts, such as destructive conflict, unfavorable working conditions, rampant political intrigue, and higher employee turnover.

The Refusal of Senior Generations to Hand over Power

The reluctance of senior generations to hand over control to the younger generations can also create conflict among family members. As they are growing up, the younger generations often feel that they are under surveillance since they are expected to take control of the business someday. They are also expected to take the field of study and jobs based on the needs of the family business, which they do not necessarily feel comfortable with, since the field of study and jobs might not match their interests and talents.

As a result, the younger generations will lose their independence and self-confidence. They also might feel frustrated and discontented since they do not feel free to express their creativity and ideas. Failure to address such concerns could undermine the sustainability of business and family relations.

Poor Communication

Communication in the family tends to be informal. Every family member tries to speak not as a partner or shareholder, but as a parent, brother, sister, and so on. Communication can be done anytime and anywhere, for example, during dinner, on vacation, or in the living room. Such conditions, if not managed carefully, could spark conflict.

Regarding communication, miscommunication and too much communication can create conflict. Many families avoid communicating honestly, citing maintaining harmony as the reason. Maintaining harmony is important; however, constructive criticism and change are also important for personal development, family relations, and business.

Growing Business and Interest

In a family business, conflicts among family members often emerge along with the company's rapid growth and development. This was the case in Nyonya Meneer, as well as YHS. The conflict started to break out at the same time the company's market share, sales, and profits were at record highs. Why does such a thing happen?

Many overseas Chinese family businesses (OCFBs) start their company to survive and get out of poverty. In such a difficult situation, it is easy to get commitment and dedication from all of the family members since they realize that the only way for them to survive is to work hard together. They usually do not care much about the compensation they receive. The patriarchal leadership makes the decision making quicker, and consensus and agreement can be reached more easily.

At the initial stage, the founder and owner has full control of the company resources, including all financial resources. The owners are also deeply involved in the company's daily operational activities, such as production, marketing, and sales activities. Owners and founders have the respected authority, based on their knowledge, information, and leadership qualities, so everyone is ready to work hard together for the company's progress.

At the beginning stage of the business, trust among the family members is higher since there is no conflict between personal and business interests. If there is such a conflict, the leader usually will mediate and resolve it without any resistance.

However, as the company grows, relations among the family members become more complicated. Information asymmetry begins to emerge, which makes it difficult for family members to get necessary information in the same degree to make the right decision. Information asymmetry occurs when one party has more or better information than the other.

After achieving success, many family businesses often feel over-confident and complacent. They often start to put personal interests over business interests. As a result, harmony within the family business is in danger.

Siblings and Cousins Rivalry

Many OCFBs still maintain the opinion that the eldest siblings are superior to the younger ones (Lee and Li, 2008). As a result, senior generations will award the eldest the highest position in the company once they retire. The younger ones, While still involved in the business, will be given lower positions. This can spark jealousy among the younger siblings, especially when they perceive the oldest sibling is less competent.

The wealth distribution can impact the relationship among siblings and cousins (Lee and Li, 2008). If one party believes the wealth distribution is unfair, he or she will become discontented, suspicious, and jealous. For example, there are family members who receive financial revenue, but contribute very little or nothing to the company's progress and performance. As a result, even a small disagreement can turn into a bitter conflict.

As the business grows and develops, more family members, including cousins, nephews, and nieces, become involved in the company. Such situations can make conflicts more complicated across families and generations, which could directly threaten the management, operation, and survival of the business. In Nyonya Meneer, conflicts involved cousins, uncles, aunts, and nephews. Charles Saerang, the current president director, got involved in three bitter conflicts with his uncle, aunts, and cousins regarding control of the company.

This conflict became even more apparent with the passing away of the patriarch. With the number of family branches increasing and the educational levels improving, the differences and conflicts within the family can intensify. If the conflicts cannot be resolved at an early stage, the conflict will worsen and be more destructive. Sometimes the conflicts even end up in court, as in the case of Nyonya Meneer.

Family Members' Unfair Demand from the Employees

Disagreement between family members and employees is usually related to trust and professionalism. Family members working in the company should act and behave professionally, as they demand the same thing from their employees.

Strong commitment and professionalism will create trust from the leaders or owners of the company. Trust is most often given to the family members working in the company. However, non-family professionals should be given full trust as well so that they can freely develop and implement their ideas to improve the company's performance. If the family business fails to do such a thing, non-family professionals will feel that they are not trusted. They will also feel that they are under constant surveillance, which makes them uncomfortable.

Company's Structure and System

Unprofessional, unfair, and nontransparent management systems and measures will create distrust among family members and non-family employees (Lee and Li, 2008). As a result, different power factions can ruin relationships and morale within the company. The decision-making process and conflicting goals in the company's structure and system can also be sources of conflict.

Conflict Management

In fact, not all conflicts in the family business are negative. Conflict has a positive impact if it improves achievement, gives a warning sign to modify the company's structure, and prevents bigger conflicts. Some conflicts can even push the company to move forward (Lee and Li, 2008). Conflict can lead to an in-depth understanding and spur profound thinking. Therefore, some win-win solutions can be found to promote better interaction and competition, and the development of the business can be more healthy and mature. Disagreement sometimes can enhance communication among family members and between family members and non-family employees, and subsequently eliminate misunderstandings and prevent destruction. Moreover, some insignificant conflicts can be easily resolved within the family, and therefore prevent an even bigger conflict. Given the nature of the conflict, a family enterprise should have an effective conflict management procedure.

Conflict management involves implementing strategies to limit the negative aspects of conflict and to increase the positive aspects of conflict at a level equal to, or higher than, where the conflict is taking place. Thomas and Kilmann (1974) suggested five conflict management strategies: Competition, Accommodation, Collaboration, Compromise, and Avoidance. Sorensen (1999) discusses each of these strategies in the context of family business.

Competition is concerned with position and winning. It is often based only on the concerns of the competitor; it does not take into account others' concerns. If the conflict involves the owner, it will likely be resolved to the owner's satisfaction. Thus, in resolving conflict, competition is not likely to fully address the many issues of business and family. Furthermore, competition is associated with a negative effect. Competition always involves one party preventing others from success so that it creates anger, stress, and distrust; so competition is not likely to build relationships or accommodate varied interests.

Accommodation is based on high concern for others and low concern for self. It ascertains others' desires and fulfills them while neglecting personal desires. Accommodation can establish a willingness to get along. Accommodation, by demonstrating supportiveness and acknowledgment of others' concerns, should contribute to good relationships (Seymor, 1993). In a family business, if all parties accommodate, conflicts can usually be resolved. However, too strong a norm of accommodation may prevent some parties from asserting themselves even on important issues. For example, a highly accommodative owner might sacrifice business success to satisfy his family or employees.

Collaboration is an approach that attempts to fully satisfy the concerns of all involved parties. Like accommodation, collaboration indicates a willingness to adapt. Collaboration is not just yielding to others' concerns, but is an active search for "win-win" solutions. However, collaboration requires time and effort on the part of participants. It also requires good interpersonal skills, including open communication, trust, and mutual support (Seymour, 1993). Collaboration contributes to desirable family outcomes, including positive relationships and cohesion. Because it requires mutual sharing and openness, it is more likely than accommodation to promote the organizational learning and adaptation needed to enhance business performance (Dyer, 1986). Thus, collaboration should significantly contribute both to family and business outcomes.

Compromise involves each party giving in to the other to find an acceptable solution. However, because something is given up, no one feels fully satisfied. Compromise may contribute to achieving desired business and family outcomes, but not to the same extent as would collaboration (Rahim, 1983).

Avoidance is the failure to address conflicts by denying that conflicts exist or simply avoiding directly discussing them. Although it limits direct confrontation, avoidance can escalate frustrations. For example, family members might avoid discussing conflicts at work but express their feelings with spouses, thus adding to overall negative feelings within the family. Too much avoidance leaves important business and family issues unresolved, which can heighten tension and limit productive action. In their study, Kaye and McCarthy (1996) found that a strategy of conflict avoidance was associated with relatively low family satisfaction, high sibling rivalry, and low mutual trust. Thus, avoidance does not contribute to positive business or family outcomes.

Avoiding Conflicts

The conflict management strategies discussed by Sorensen (1999) apparently assume that conflicts in family business have already emerged. However, efforts can still be taken to avoid any conflict before it has a negative impact.

For a family enterprise, it is important to recognize any warning signs that a conflict could break out. These warning signs include the following:

1. Complaints regarding equality and fairness, whether from family members or non-family employees.
2. Family members making instructions, decisions, and statements that contradict each other. This situation makes employees confused and uncomfortable.
3. An inability to reach consensus, even for less important matters.
4. Lack of, or even no, clear vision from the family business owner.
5. Family members lack understanding regarding their roles and responsibilities in the business.
6. Family members start leaving the business because they do not feel emotional bonding among themselves.
7. Nepotism, a recruitment policy prioritizing family members without considering their competence. This will create discontent among employees.
8. Senior generations still intervene in day-to-day business activities although they have announced their retirement.
9. The absence of an independent party on the company's board of directors, as well as the absence of any open discussions between management and the company's owners.
10. Lack of succession planning.
11. Difficulties in recruiting and retaining managers from outside family.

A family business should be aware of the warning signs and then take steps before the conflicts get out of control. Here are things a family business must do to avoid any destructive conflicts:

1. *Creating a Fair Human Resource Policy*

In recruiting family members to work in the company, the business leaders should accept only those who have the required competence. Compensation for family members has to be based on business values instead of family values. A family business must create a fair compensation policy, aiming to achieve the company's goals and objectives.

The job performance of family members working in the company should be evaluated only according to their professionalism and contribution to the business. Non-family members should also be given a chance and more freedom to evaluate family members. This must be done to avoid any bias

It is important to create career development planning for family members. Career paths for family members should be aligned with overall company goals and objectives, both in the short-term and long-term. Family members whose talent, interest, and needs don't match with the company's goals and objectives should reconsider their involvement in the business. However, they can still be given ownership status and claim their family assets to be invested outside of the company.

2. *Fostering Open Communication*

Open communication among family members and between family members and outsiders should be encouraged to eliminate misunderstanding and information obstacles. This includes building effective communication systems. This communication, formal or informal, face-to-face or conducted by a third party, may help improve the quality of communication in family enterprises (Lee and Li, 2008). As part of fostering open communication, family meetings discussing issues regarding the business should be done on a regular basis if necessary. Family members should also be honest when managing the business, including problems they are facing, expectations, and plans for the future.

3. *Preparing Succession Planning*

Succession planning enables senior generations to comfortably hand over the power to the younger ones when the time comes. While at the same time, younger generations can take over the control of the company without being afraid of any intervention from their parents. By enjoying great privileges and authority, the younger generations will be able to develop and implement their ideas and creativity so that they can prepare the company in facing up to new challenges.

4. *Governing Family Members*

One way to avoid negative conflict is to limit the role of each family member working in the business, including siblings and cousins. Another issue that should be addressed thoroughly is the distribution of revenue, ownership, and property among family members. For this purpose, the family can ask for third-party help so it can get an objective perspective. Apart from business matters, it is useful if family members spend some time together so that they can foster mutual understanding and build closer relationships.

For a growing company, creating good organizational structure and systems is very important in order to make the company more advanced, while at the same time it must keep observing changing developments.

Conflict Resolution in Chinese Family Businesses: A Different Approach

Managing and avoiding conflict among family members in a family business is important indeed. However, Chinese family businesses have different views and approaches regarding family conflicts. One view and approach has to do with the good name of the family. In Chinese tradition, promoting and maintaining family glory and reputation is important, meaning that Chinese family businesses will do everything to save face. Many Chinese people believe that when they are involved in a bitter conflict, their good name will be tarnished, and building a good name requires time and painstaking effort. This will make external parties such as customers, suppliers, and members of the networks (*guanxi*) doubt their reliability and credibility in sustaining their businesses. As a result, making business deals and agreements will become more difficult. Restoring such credibility often requires a large effort and is costly, particularly for businesses and individuals that already have a strong image.

Because of the strong desire to save face and to build and maintain a good name, many Chinese family businesses tend to hide conflicts that take place among family members. One way to do this is to act as if there is no disagreement or dispute among family members. For example, all family members might appear together in public to show that they are united and have a harmonious relationship and are ready to make the family business thrive. Another purpose for doing this is to crush the competitor. Covering up disputes and disagreements can also be handled by intensifying promotions regarding company products and activities.

Does this mean that they don't care about the conflict? Not necessarily. They realize that disagreement and dispute exist. Nevertheless, they believe that everything will be settled naturally. For religious people, they say that they will pray and leave the problem to God. For those who are involved in conflict, they still try to resolve the dispute. It seems that they have an unwritten agreement not to show their disagreement in public and in front of other family members, although they still talk behind each other's backs. How they discuss the problem depends on their education.

What Andrew Cherng, the founder of Panda Express, has experienced, is interesting. Andrew acknowledges the difficulty of running a business while keeping family harmony. Working with his wife, Peggy, caused a strain in their marriage. To help save their relationship, Cherng persuaded Peggy to hire Thomas Davin, a former Marine captain and Taco Bell operations boss, to replace her. Nevertheless, at the beginning, Peggy resisted Andrew's idea of bringing in an outside president with restaurant industry experience to replace her. Ultimately, they agreed to try again and made the hire and Peggy was happy about the decision.

Family strain in Chinese family businesses is common. For the older generation, divorce is taboo.

Chapter 5

The Succession Conundrums

Succession is one of the most important issues in a family firm, since it will decide the company's sustainability in the future. Some family firms thrive after the succession; unfortunately many more decline after the founder passes away or retires. Overseas Chinese family firms are no exception. Take Kam Lun Tai, for example. Once a successful trade, remittance, and tin mining firm, the company faded after the death of its founder, K.L. Lee, in June 1936. H.S. Lee, the son of K.L. Lee, was chosen by his father to lead Kam Lun Tai, but focused more on his political career in Malaysia. One younger brother did not want to take a leading role in the business, while the other younger brother knew little about the business.

Succession should not simply be viewed as replacing the older generation with the younger one as top management. Succession relates to the company's strategic planning, career development, the role of the older generation after leaving his or her leadership post, and the commitment of the younger generation to the family and business. Succession can also affect the company's relationship with external parties, such as suppliers, customers, and financial institutions. These parties want to see who will be in charge after the senior generation is no longer at the helm of the business and then decide whether they can maintain their cooperation and relationship with the company.

Succession Planning Conundrums

Because of its strategic importance, a family firm should prepare a succession plan. The successful transfer of power from the older generation to the younger one depends on the clarity of the succession planning. In a family business, succession planning is a process of identifying and developing family members, particularly the younger generations, who have the potential to fill leadership positions in the company. Succession planning will help the company maintain its stability and performance, and also can maintain family harmony. Activities in succession planning include formulating and sharing the company and family vision after the founder leaves the company; selecting, educating, and training the future successors and top management; preparing the process of transferring power from the senior generation to the younger one; preparing the estate plan, including detailed explanations regarding the process of transferring ownership from senior generations to the younger ones; preparing changes in organizational structure; and educating the family so that they can understand their rights, responsibilities, and roles in the future.

Succession planning, however, does not always run smoothly. The following factors can work to impede succession planning.

Resistance from the Senior Generation

Many senior generations resist succession planning. Even if they have a plan it is often inconsistently implemented. One example is a family business founder who chooses his eldest son as his successor, but refuses to provide the coaching and training his son needs. On one hand, nominating his son as his successor shows his commitment to the company's sustainability, but on the other hand, his refusal to provide training and coaching for his son's personal development shows that the founder still wants to have full control over the company.

Senior generations often refuse to plan the succession because they associate succession with old age, declining health, or even death. They do not want to talk about death, especially when they are still healthy and strong. For many, talking about death is considered a hostile act.

Senior generations also resist succession planning because it means they will have to relinquish their power in the firm. Remember that many people decide to become entrepreneurs because they want to have influence and control over others. Relinquishing their power means relinquishing their entire life. To demonstrate their power, they tend to make themselves irreplaceable by not delegating authority and intervening in daily business activities. They also often exaggerate the threat of the company's demise if they are not involved.

Another reason why founders refuse to engage in succession planning is the fear of losing an important part of their identity. Senior generations are afraid that people will underestimate and isolate them because they are no longer in power.

For senior generations, the business is part of their identity. Whether the younger generation can maintain their legacy concerns them. Another impediment for succession planning is jealousy by senior generations of their children.

Many senior generations do not make a plan for succession because they feel that their children are not interested in running the business. They also find it difficult to decide which one of their children deserves to replace them. They also worry that conflict will break out among the children. Resistance to succession planning also sometimes comes from the founder's spouse, who does not want to lose his or her identity as the spouse of a business leader.

The willingness of senior generations is required for successful succession planning, and the emotional needs and feelings of insecurity should be addressed. The family must realize and understand that it is difficult and painful for the senior generation to leave their business. However, founders who have interests or hobbies outside the business will feel more comfortable developing a succession plan. It also reduces the feeling of uncertainty and fear of losing their connection with the business after they retire. The activities should be meaningful both for the senior generations and for other people. For example, getting involved in social activities will enhance the reputation of senior generations. Fortunately, many founders of successful overseas Chinese family businesses have done this. People like Ciputra, Mochtar Riady, Eka Tjipta Widjaja (Indonesia), Robert Kuok, Lee Shin Cheng (Malaysia), and Henry Sy (Philippines) have set up foundations or institutions that specialize in non-business activities. Most of these foundations or institutions specialize in social, health, and education activities.

After their retirement, the senior generations can also share their experiences about running a family business by writing books and giving lectures. This could be a benefit to other people, particularly to families interested to running and developing their own businesses.

If this is not enough, the senior generation can do small business activities so that they can still manage and influence other people, although on a smaller scale. The number of employees in this new business should also be small.

Poor Communication among Family Members

In most family businesses, there are always a few family members who do not know how to express their feelings. This makes them feel frustrated, unproductive, and unwilling to take risks. In family and cultural traditions, family members are taught not to express their feelings if it can hurt other people's feelings, although they might have certain expectations.

Poor communication is also related to the inability to appreciate differences. Differences are important to create a more dynamic and interesting life. By citing the importance of preserving family harmony, family members tend to avoid discussing differences in the family business.

Family members must enhance their communication skills so that they can communicate their ideas, opinions, and feelings clearly. This can be done, for example, by completing some communication training. This will make them feel more self-confident and enable them to express their ideas assertively.

Rejection from the Younger Generation

The younger generations are often reluctant to succeed their parents in family business because they do not want to get involved in conflict, are not given a chance, are not interested in the family business, or do not have the competence.

The successor of a family business, whether the first, second, or third generation, always faces different challenges compared with his or her predecessor regarding managing the family relationship and managing the business. For example, the second generation has to make adjustments only with the first generation, and he or she also has a stronger emotional bond with the business founded by the parents. But when the third or fourth generation assumes power, there might be more family members and professionals joining the company. These people often have different goals, interests, ideas, insights, and perceptions, which could create conflict. To anticipate any conflict, all family members must make an agreement regarding responsibilities, authorities, rights, and obligations for every person across multiple generations. This includes career path, wealth, and estate planning.

Ciputra, the founder of Ciputra Development, one of Indonesia's leading property companies, is one example. He has prepared a written family contract. The contract reveals that if a family member wants to leave the company, he or she cannot sell his or her stake without the consent of other family members. If he or she wants to establish a company that specializes in the same field, the family member can serve only as a director, not a commissioner. According to Ciputra, such a contract has to be drafted at a time when the family members are still healthy and strong. Every month or two there will be a family meeting. This meeting is also held with the other professionals.

Younger generations are often given only a limited chance to prove their ability. At the same time, senior generations often don't recognize the maturity and ability of the younger ones. So, it's not surprising when younger generations feel that they do not receive enough appreciation from their seniors, and they want their achievements to be valued. As a result, they tend to be apathetic regarding succession planning and the company's future. Family members must realize the importance of appreciating each other, because the non-financial reward is as important as the financial one.

If one of the younger generation is not interested in working in the family business or succeeding the senior one, he or she should be given the freedom to choose. If he or she doesn't have the competence, recruiting professionals from outside the family is the best option.

Impediments from Non-Family Professionals and Outsiders

Non-family professional managers often perceive that the younger generation lacks the entrepreneurial skills and spirit compared to the founder. Other impediments come from external parties such as customers, suppliers, and financial institutions, which prefer dealing with the founder rather than trusting the successor. To overcome this issue, the competence of the successor needs to be continuously developed.

Succession in Overseas Chinese Family Businesses: Influence of Confucian Values

Resistance to succession planning could come from the older generation, younger generation, non-family professionals, or external parties, who feel that their individual interests could be threatened should the succession takes place. However, this notion is based on the assumption that a family business embraces culture resembling the characteristics of individualistic societies, as suggested by Hofstede (1991). To the contrary, Chinese society, largely influenced by Confucian values, is one of the most collectivist societies. Table 5.1 summarizes the differences between individualistic and collectivist societies, which are relevant to the succession issue.

In overseas Chinese family businesses (OCFBs), Confucian values have significant influence. Yan and Sorensen (2006) have suggested that the more a Chinese family business adheres to Confucian values and principles, the less resistance there will be to the succession. Let us take a look at some basic Confucian teachings.

In Confucian teaching, the family is more important than any individual member and harmony is the most important value for family members. A family member must put aside his or her interest for the

Table 5.1 Succession Issues and Cultural Barriers

Individualistic Society	Collectivist Society
Focus on self and to some extent one's extended family	Consider extended family and remain loyal to the predecessor
Success is accounted to self	Success is for the family and determined by the social network one belongs to
Self-expression for higher recognition and openness	Maintaining harmony to create balance, self-expression within certain lines
Employer–employee relationship is transactional	Employer–employee is long-term relationship; those who stayed became part of the family
Individual performance as the basis for hiring and promotion	Fitness to group and acceptability is the key for hiring and promotion
Individual interest can be pursued	Group interest will be prioritized
Free expression of opinion	Opinions are determined by the group
Self-actualization and recognition is the ultimate goal	Harmony and balance is the ultimate goal

Adapted from Yan and Sorensen (2006), which is extracted from Hofstede (1991)

sake of the family. Each member also has to be ready to sacrifice himself or herself for the family.

The parent–child relationship is the most emphasized in Confucian teaching. The nature of the parent–child relationship is reciprocal, where children serve their parents with filial piety and submission, and parents treat their children with kindness and care. Filial piety is shown by a high level of devotion, including affection, respect, duty, and obedience (Yan and Sorensen, 2006). Parents still exert their influence over children, even after the children become financially independent and have their own family. Parents must take care of their children when they are young, and children must take care of their parents in their old age. Parents also give their children guidance throughout their life.

Children must also respect and obey senior members of the family, while older members must be kind to the younger ones. When the father dies, the eldest son takes the leadership role and becomes the decision maker.

Outside the family, the relationship between one person and another is based on two principles, hierarchical relationships and trustworthiness (Yan and Sorensen, 2006). In hierarchical relationships, the ruled is expected to be submissive to the ruler. At the same time, the ruler is expected to be kind and caring to the ruled. This hierarchical relationship can be discovered between superior and subordinates, employers and employee, teachers and students, and so forth. Trustworthiness is apparently based on a famous Confucian golden rule, which states *What you do not wish for yourself, do not do to others.* This principle becomes the basis for building mutual trust and reducing opportunistic behavior.

These Confucian values greatly influence succession in OCFBs. Since in the Confucian tradition parents are obliged to give their children guidelines and advice, even after the children take over the leadership of the family business they still go to the father to ask for advice. This makes resistance to succession low because the father still plays an important role in the business and often plays an active role in planning the succession. He also doesn't have to worry about losing financial support because Confucian tradition teaches children to support and take care of their parents in their old age.

Senior generations often face difficulties when deciding which of their children deserves the top leadership post. This is rarely the case for many OCFBs though, because in these companies, sons have exclusive rights and privileges over daughters, and elder brothers are likely to take the highest executive position.

Younger generations often resist succession planning because they feel that the opportunities and rewards in the family business do not match their personal and career aspirations. However, Confucian tradition could reduce such resistance because it teaches children strong loyalty and obligation to the family, as well as filial piety and submission to parental decisions. If the children ultimately work outside of the family business, the decision is made after consulting with their family, particularly their parents. Parents might agree that the children will have better opportunities to develop themselves if they work outside of the family business. So, it is not always the children themselves making the decision.

At the same time, most children believe that whatever decision is made by their parents is the best one for the entire family. They also believe that their parents will treat them with kindness, care, and respect, so any decision made by their parents regarding succession will be accepted.

Successful succession planning depends on the family's commitment; the quality of the relationships between the senior generation, the younger generation, and the non-family professionals; and relationships among family members. However, since Confucianism teaches harmony, mutual trust, and compliance with the leader, the family commitment and the relationship among family members and between family members and professional managers should remain strong.

Lansberg (1988) suggested that resistance to succession sometimes comes from family business managers. Such resistance could be based more on reluctance to shift from a personal relationship with the founder to a more formal relationship with the successor, a change in employment due to a change in organizational structure, or fear of loss of autonomy and influence.

However, in OCFBs influenced by Confucian values, informal and personal relationships between family members and non-family professionals are common (Lee, 1996). This is mostly because employees are either friends or family or referred by friends or family. Most successors grow up in an environment that is informal and personal. Since childhood they already have had a good relationship with the firm's employees, especially the senior ones. This situation creates less or even no resistance to succession from non-family managers.

Environment can also influence succession in a family firm. In the case of OCFBs, *guanxi* is important; it enables many businesses to survive the harsh environment. Many Chinese firms rely on *guanxi* to get things done; for example, when a new business is proposed, a Chinese business will first consult its network of relatives, friends, and other Chinese businesses (Richter, 2002). Overseas Chinese family business leaders also use *guanxi* to build cooperation and identify business opportunities.

Members of the *guanxi* network believe that their own survival and prosperity are tied to that of the entire network (Yan and Sorensen, 2006). Smooth and successful succession in the network will guarantee the long-term survival and stability of the entire network. If the succession fails, the stability and even the existence of the network will be at risk. So, it is not surprising that members of the network help each other address and resolve succession issues.

Preparing the Next Generation of Leaders in Overseas Chinese Family Businesses

Overcoming resistance to succession alone does not guarantee the company's long-term growth and stability. To be able to successfully lead the business, younger generations need help from their parents.

Developing Leadership Qualities

Smooth transition of power will be meaningless if it merely produces weak leadership in the hands of the younger generation. This is one of the issues facing many Chinese family businesses. The successors are not thought of as having quality leadership compared to their predecessors. They lack vision, do not have the enthusiasm to lead the business, do not have the courage to take risks, are not good at identifying opportunities, are not able to accept responsibility, and so forth. However, senior generations might also be responsible for the weak leadership. Weak leadership occurs because the senior generations fail to develop the leadership qualities of the younger ones.

Many OCFBs have a long-term vision. This creates advantages. They have the flexibility to arrange their schedule without having to be afraid of stock market pressure. As a result, they can concentrate on activities whose impact will only be seen in the long term, such as satisfying and retaining customers, developing their human resources, and promoting innovation. This long-term vision can also be capitalized on to prepare the next generation.

The best way to start developing quality leadership is to create bonds based on mutual trust and respect. A good example would be the Toula Corporation. Toula Corporation is an apparel enterprise with design teams on three continents, with their headquarters and a distribution center in Dallas, Texas, and production facilities in mainland China. The company was established in 1986 by Eddie Wang and his wife, Ming

Wang. Both are Taiwanese natives. In 2003, the couple's older son, Steven, joined the company and helped to significantly spur its growth. Three years later, his brother Eric also joined Toula and now manages real estate and oversees a retail operation. In one interview, Eddie said that he has a good relationship with his children; since his sons were little they have been very close. Steven added that there had to be a lot of trust in things and that he has a lot of respect for his parents because of what they have done for the company.

Instilling a Sense of Belonging to the Business

Parents also must instill a sense of belonging, as suggested by Charles Saerang from Nyonya Meneer Indonesia. This should be started by promoting the work ethos and teaching the children to love what the parents do. Charles often has discussions with his children when they are in a comfortable situation. He chooses a topic that encourages them to expand their knowledge. He suggests that this has to be done regularly.

Andrew Tan from the Alliance Global Group Inc., Philippines, said that he often has lunch with his son, Kevin Tan. Sometimes he uses the time they are together to give Kevin a few words of wisdom. (Andrew Tan said that he would like it better if Kevin took what he told him to heart.)

Andrew Tan also said that as a father he believes that it is his job is to make his children interested in the business. If they're passionate about it, they will put in the hard work without feeling stressed.

Transferring Knowledge to the Younger Generation

Parents must transfer their knowledge to their children. The successor needs knowledge regarding the company and industry, and needs skills to enhance his competence. For the younger generation to gain knowledge and skills, the senior generation must act as a mentor. In the learning process, parents must let children make mistakes to a certain extent, but after the parents see that their children have gained adequate skills, knowledge, and experience, they feel that they can now be trusted. In Toula Corporation, when Eddie saw that his son, Steven, could handle the business, he gave him more freedom; business has increased rapidly since Steven joined the company.

Robin Tan, the son of Vincent Tan, from Berjaya, Malaysia, said that he was being groomed and trained to take over the Berjaya Group. "Being the eldest in the family, a lot of responsibilities and expectations have been placed on me to lead the family and perform well for this company," Robin said. After graduating from a school in the United Kingdom (UK) in 1995, Robin immediately joined the group as an executive. In 1997, he was made the group's general manager of corporate affairs. In 2003, he was appointed CEO of Berjaya Land. However, it wasn't until 15 years later that Robin became the CEO of Berjaya Group, effective January 1, 2011.

Promoting Entrepreneurial Spirit among Younger Generations

The second and third generations of family business leaders often consider themselves managers, not entrepreneurs. It is the founder who is considered the entrepreneur or pioneer and who can realize his business ideas. However, it is important for the senior generation to instill the entrepreneurial spirit in the mind of their successor. By doing so, new opportunities could be identified and capitalized on.

Risk is perceived differently by the senior and younger generations. Senior generations tend to be more conservative, while the younger ones tend to be more creative, tolerant, and courageous in taking risk. However, the risk taken must be calculated. The good news is that in many Chinese family businesses, both senior and younger generations have great entrepreneurial skills and spirit.

Giving Everyone a Chance Regardless of Gender

In many Chinese family businesses, sons are privileged over daughters to take the leadership post. However, many women have proven themselves to be great leaders. Peggy Tsiang Cherng, chief executive and co-chair of Panda Restaurant Group, is one example. Born to Chinese parents in Burma, Peggy Tsiang Cherng came to the United States to attend college and stayed to pursue a career in engineering. With a doctorate in electrical engineering, Cherng spent years as part of technical teams at high-tech firms, such as McDonnell Douglas and Comtal-3M. But in 1982, Cherng left the tech world to join her husband,

Andrew Cherng, who, along with his father, had opened the successful Panda Inn, in Pasadena, California. The Panda Inn was a casual-dining concept featuring Mandarin and Szechuan cuisine. Now Panda Restaurant Group—based in Rosemead, California—has more than 700 Panda Express locations in 36 states. Peggy Tsiang Cherng is known for her role in establishing the company's vision, mission, and value statements. Since women can be great leaders and managers, every young person in a family business should be given an equal chance to take the leadership post, regardless of gender.

Another example is The Hour Glass Limited (THG). THG grew from a local company in Singapore with just a single retail outlet to become a publicly listed company with 13 retail outlets in Singapore, Malaysia, Thailand, Hong Kong, and Australia, specializing in the retailing and distributorship of luxury Swiss watches. It is run by Jannie Tay and her husband, Henry Tay, together with active involvement of third-generation family members, particularly in this instance, Michael Tay, the son of Henry and Jannie, who is now the executive director of THG. THG was founded in 1979 by Jannie and Henry, when they formed THG together with Metro Holdings Ltd. (Metro) after Jannie helped her husband and his family in their family's watch business. Jannie revolutionized the watch business by creating a new image as a luxury watch retailer and distributor. THG expanded its operations in the late 1980s to broaden its customer base and to cater to a wide range of markets. THG also established outlets in Australia, Malaysia, Hong Kong, Indonesia, and Brunei.

Yuwadee Chirathivat, a member of the Chirathivat family from Central Group, Thailand, is now the president of Central Department Store, which is operated under Central Retail Corporation (CRC). CRC is the largest retailer in Thailand. The company's huge properties offer everything from fine dining and entertainment to jewelry and even automobiles. Yuwadee joined Central in 1981, the year before it opened its first department store. Yuwadee has expanded Central to a dozen prime Bangkok locations, other key Thai cities, and China.

In the Philippines, there is Teresita Sy-Coson, the daughter of Henry Sy, Sr., the founder of SM Prime Holdings, Inc. or SM Prime, the largest shopping mall and retail operator in the Philippines. She is now a vice chairman of SM Investment Corp. (SMIC), the parent company of

SM Prime Holdings, Inc. For more than two decades she was in charge of SM's retail operations, which include the largest and most profitable group of department stores in the Philippines, and since 2007 she has been chairwoman of SMIC's majority-owned Banco de Oro Unibank, which bought Equitable, the bank she used to visit with her grandfather. She is also an advisor to SM Prime.

In 1972, Sy-Coson was asked by her father to open the first department store in Manila. The 20,000-square-meter space was considered large at the time and introduced new merchandise as well as fresh concepts in store design and displays. As Sy-Coson's career evolved, so did the family empire. In 1985, she helped her father launch the group's first shopping mall, SM North Edsa. In 1990, Sy-Coson became president of the SM Department Stores unit, now part of the SM Retail group. At the time it had fewer than 10 stores. By the time she stepped down in 2010 that number had more than quadrupled to 42.

As the eldest of his six children, Sy-Coson is often referred to in the media as her father's heir apparent, but she sees things differently. She points out that she is not the only one running things, that all of her siblings are involved as well. She views her role as more of a manager. "I was not meant to lead the group. Even now I am not leading; I maintain the core." Lance Gokongwei, president of JG Summit Group, a competitor in retail and malls, says that Teresita Sy-Coson is very well regarded within and outside the Philippines and she has proven over time that she's a capable successor to her father. Lance Gokongwei also said that Teresita Sy-Coson's ability to approach situations from different perspectives is a huge strength. She has high standards, is very detailed, has a very strategic viewpoint, and is very down to earth.

Because there is so much proof that women have the ability to lead businesses, choosing successors based on gender is no longer relevant. In choosing someone to fill a leadership position, Ciputra does not take gender into consideration. As long as a person has the required qualifications, he or she should be given the chance.

Giving Every Member of the Younger Generation a Chance

Before deciding who will fill the top leadership post, parents should give every child an equal chance to prove him- or herself. Francis Yeoh Sock

Ping (Francis Yeoh) from YTL is one example. Yeoh's children, nephews, and nieces, as well as non-family professionals, now lead business units in YTL. Non-family professionals include Kemmy Tan Peck Mun, who was appointed CEO of YTL Land and Development Berhad in 2008. There is also Wing K. Lee, who was appointed CEO YTL Communication Sdn Bhd. Yeoh's children, nephews, and nieces have to compete with these professionals to be the best. When they succeed, one of them will be the CEO of the whole group.

Suthichart Chirathivat from Central Group, Thailand, explained that Central Group prioritizes the members of the family council when selecting a manager. Their qualifications and performance will be assessed and evaluated. If they do not meet the required qualifications, they will be placed in another business unit or be given an easier job. One of the benefits when appointing a family member to a certain job is that he or she is already familiar with the business and the family. However, he or she will be difficult to terminate because it will create uneasiness.

Chances must be given to all children, regardless of age. In Salim Group, Indonesia, Anthony Salim is not the eldest son. He has one older brother, Albert. However, by virtue of hard work and a proven track record, Anthony emerged as the next family leader of the Salims.

The Next Generations: Dealing with Challenges

The development of a family business starts from the founder's immediate family. Next, as the business grows, the second generation and extended family start to join. The number of non-family employees also increases.

The joining of more family members and non-family professionals indicates the ability of a family business to flourish, thanks mostly to the senior generation. However, at the same time, the company also faces new challenges. Nowadays, the challenges include globalization, competition, advanced technology, climate change, corporate social responsibility, and economic turbulence.

Most founders and leaders of Chinese family businesses want their business to survive and thrive although they will no longer be at the helm. To achieve this, they depend on the ability of the younger generations.

Younger generations have advantages as compared to senior ones. Many of them graduate from the best universities in the world, have a wide network both in the country and abroad, and have support from their parents. They also do not have to start from the very beginning because their parents have built the company's strong foundation. Their challenge is to capitalize on the advantages. Nevertheless, younger generations admit that this is not an easy job. For Kevin Tan, Alliance Global Group Inc., Philippines, it's not easy to follow in his dad's revered footsteps: "The companies that he spent his entire life creating are his best legacy to us. We are compelled yet honored and determined to carry on what he has started. The fact that these companies were built from practically nothing is our biggest motivation to succeed and continue his lifelong achievements."

Deciding to Join or Not to Join

The younger generations must decide whether they want to join the family business and succeed their parents. This is surely not an easy decision because they have to consider their obligation to the family, sibling rivalry, and an unfriendly reception because of their status as the children of the founder. In Chinese tradition the children are expected to preserve the family legacy, including the family business. On the one hand, it would be better if the younger generations consulted their parents and siblings. On the other hand, the parents should give the children discretion whether they want to join the company or not. Richard Eu, the CEO of Eu Yan Sang, in one interview said that the children will not be forced to enter the family business if they are not interested. Kenny Yap of Qian Hu said that the future generations should be given a chance to decide for themselves whether they are interested in joining the family business.

Teresita Sy-Coson plans to give her three children, ranging in age from their late teens to mid–20s, a choice. "There are just two milestones: At 25, they have to start working. At 30, they have to make a choice for their future, whether to build their own career or join the company," she says.

Parents do not have to force the younger generations to join the family business. Nevertheless, they can give encouragement. We can learn from Henry Sy, Jr., the son of Henry Sy, Sr., and the brother of Teresita Sy-Coson. He believes the younger generation cannot be forced to go into the family business, but they can certainly be encouraged. By encouragement, he means taking his children with him on business trips and exposing them early on to the fringe privileges of being a successful entrepreneur. He also shared that this method has started to work wonders with his kids, judging by his eldest child's growing interest in the business. Today, Henry Sy, Jr. is the vice chairman and chief executive officer of SM Development Corporation.

If the younger generations decide to work in the family business and subsequently take over the leadership, they must first evaluate the decision-making process, the priority both for short and long term, changes regarding family relationships, the morale of employees, and the company's vision and mission.

Implementing Modern Management Principles

As the family business flourishes, the younger generations must implement modern management principles. They must create a proper organizational structure and system aimed at promoting professionalism. The first ten months after Charles Saerang was appointed as president director of Nyonya Meneer, he completely restructured and streamlined the executive management and the human resource department. The reporting lines were untangled and job descriptions were made transparent.

Fortunately, nowadays many younger generations in Chinese family businesses are trained professionally and are open to the new management theories, which they combine with Chinese cultural values such as frugality, modesty, and persistence. Furthermore, they modify these values in the context of the volatile business environment. They are also guided by professional values and standards that are inspired by the management examples practiced by the non-family professional executives. The younger generations of the family work diligently in maintaining entrepreneurial function in their firms. They are also able to change traditional Chinese values, which did not put high trust in non-family members, and overcome their feelings of distrust regarding the administrative responsibilities. They are able to delegate these responsibilities to non-family professional managers.

Staying Humble

Successful younger generations in a family business never stop learning. They are willing to listen to others, as well as appreciating their efforts and point of view. They are considerate even though they are the children of the founder. They never underestimate other people even though they graduated from the best universities in the world. They behave well to senior generations and show respect for their dedication and hard work.

Teresita Sy-Coson could be one example. According to Lydia C. King, who worked with Sy-Coson at BDO as first vice president for technology, "She was a very dynamic but practical hands-on leader. She exhibits a democratic management style allowing officers to express themselves and participate in the decision-making process."

Managing Conflicts

Within the family, if the younger generations are able to manage the conflict potential well, the joining of other family members in the business could enhance harmony. A sense of togetherness in running the business will strengthen the family bond. Conflict emerges because there are differences regarding personal goals, family goals, and business goals. If not managed well, conflict can damage the family firm. To avoid conflict, the family needs to define any role, right, obligation, and responsibility for each person in the business. Family meetings discussing the company's current condition and future should be conducted.

Delegating More Authority

The younger generations must address the leadership issue after the seniors leave the business. At an early stage, leadership in the family business tends to be informal. The founder doesn't like to create organizational structures and systems because he feels that they will limit the company's flexibility. There is still no strict separation between company and personal issues. At this stage, the founder doesn't like to depend on people other than the family members, particularly regarding strategic decisions. He does not even want to involve the younger generations yet. The power to make decisions lies in the hands of the founder.

However, as the company thrives, marked by increases in income, profits, assets, market share, customers, employees, operating location, operation complexity, and family members joining the company, "the one-show model" in which the top leader holds all the power can no longer be maintained. The younger generations must delegate authority, both to the other family members and to non-family professionals. The latter consist of people with high competence and they will not be satisfied if not given more opportunities to develop themselves. Roles and responsibilities for each employee and family member should be defined clearly. This requires an understanding regarding the strengths and weaknesses of each person working in the company. Also important is fair recruitment, selection, compensation, and performance evaluations.

Robin Tan recognizes the need to empower the talent in Berjaya Group, of which he thinks there is plenty. And one way to empower your talent is to delegate more authority.

Finding Work Experience Outside the Family Business

Working outside the family business before joining the firm will give valuable lessons to the younger generations. Successors joining the family business after gaining work experience from outside the firm will be welcomed by employees. By working outside the family business, they will gain valuable insight regarding basic operations of a business, which in turn enhances their credibility so that they can do their job better.

It will be useful if the successor can start his career in the family business at the bottom, although it doesn't have to be that way. It will give the successor more understanding about each function and task as well as the challenges each employee faces.

Michael Riady, the grandson of Mochtar Riady, the founder of Lippo Group in Indonesia, is one example. Prior to joining Lippo group, he worked at Fidelity Inverstment, a multinational financial services corporation, before moving to Manatt, Phelps, and Philip, a Los Angeles-based law firm. However, as he joined Lippo Group, he had to pass the learning stage before holding a top leadership position. He had to show that he was not just the grandson of Mochtar Riady. In 2006, he took care of the exhibition room at Mall Metropolis. As time passed, his responsibility increased and he started to handle bigger property projects. In 2007, he became the CEO of the St. Moritz & Lippo Shopping Malls Group. Currently, he is the CEO of Shopping Malls Group and Mixed-Use Development at PT Lippo Karawaci Tbk.

Another example is Quek Kon Sean. He is the son of Quek Leng Chan, the founder of Hong Leong Financial Group in Malayisa. Prior to joining the Hong Leong Financial Group on December 1, 2005, he served as an analyst in the Investment Banking Division of Goldman Sachs International, London, from 2002 to 2003. Then he served as an Analyst of Debt Capital Markets at HSBC, London, from 2003 to 2004, and Management Executive of HL Management Co. Sdn Bhd, from August 2004 to November 2005. Quek Kon Sean has been non-independent and non-executive director of Camerlin Group Bhd since May 17, 2005, and HLG Capital Berhad since February 28, 2006. He has been director for Hong Leong Bank Bhd since July 10, 2006. He also serves as a director of Hong Leong Islamic Bank Berhad and Hong Leong Assurance Berhad.

Rayvin Tan Yeong Sheik, the son of Vincent Tan from Berjaya, Malaysia, has been an executive director of the Board of Berjaya Corporation Berhad since September 2005. Rayvin Tan Yeong Sheik also serves as executive director of Berjaya Sports Toto Berhad. He joined the Berjaya Group of Companies in May 2001 as senior manager, Corporate Affairs of Kota Raya Development Sdn Bhd and Noble Circle Management Sdn Bhd. Rayvin Tan Yeong Sheik was subsequently appointed to the position of general manager, Corporate Affairs of Sports Toto Malaysia Sdn Bhd in February 2002. He participated in vocational training as a research intern with Jardine Fleming and Merrill Lynch & Co./Smith Zain Securities. During his vocational training, he was involved in the field of research covering the various sectors of property, commodities, telecommunications, and transport.

Prior to joining Bangkok Bank, Chartsiri Sophonpanich worked at Citibank in New York. He gained extensive experience at both operational and managerial levels in various departments at Bangkok Bank, including Foreign Exchange Trading, Marketing, Treasury, Investment Banking Group, and International Banking Group before being appointed President on December 1, 1994.

Ciputra requires the third generation to have at least three years of working experience outside the family business before they can join. Once they join the company, they will be placed in a position according to their experience and competence.

Being a Change Agent

Younger generations in Chinese family businesses have to be the change agents. Change is difficult in a family business. However, younger generations have to convince employees and family members about the importance of change. To be able to do that, they must be able to show enthusiasm to win support from employees and family members. They must not become complacent because of past successes. Instead, they have to be vigilant to any change that could have an impact on the business. Excessive pride will trigger the organization's potential weaknesses, even at a time when the organization is at peak performance. In an established condition, there is also potential for destruction that a leader should be made aware of. Remember that our reason to exist is not to relive the past and maintain what we have achieved, but to pave the way for new life in the future.

Robin Tan of Berjaya, Malaysia, once said, "We have to learn to adopt and change according to market demand. And this is where I come in to complement my father." He apparently understands that different situations will require different management styles.

In order to run a change program successfully, younger generations of family business leaders must remember the laws of change and comply with them. Those laws are: *Law of Native, Law of Chaos*, and *Law of Eden*.

Law of Native means that any change program has to involve all organization members. No-one outside the organization can force changes to happen without the involvement of the organization members.

Law of Chaos means that any change will always create inconvenience. There will be resistance, particularly from those who feel that their power or income will be reduced and lost. There will be suggestions or remarks that could break the spirit, such as: "This change has no clear direction," "The new approach is confusing," "This change reduces performance," and so on. Resistance can hinder change if it is ignored and not managed well. Therefore, it is very important to understand the reasons behind any change resistance. The reasons are: lack of understanding regarding the importance of change and how it should be made, lack of time to participate in the change effort, the feeling of inability to do the new tasks, and disagreement regarding the change when people think that the change is a mistake. The organization must find the right strategy to control such inconveniences.

Law of Eden means that any change program needs support from a person with high competence and commitment who can act as a positive role model. Followers surely want to know the benefits of a change if it succeeds, despite its risks and complexity.

Younger generations in the family business must realize that change is a process. Therefore, the most basic question that has to be answered in the change management strategy is: *Toward what end?* This is called *vision of change.* A leader has the responsibility to formulate and share his or her vision with all organization members. He or she has to become a "merchant of hope" to all followers. A leader has to communicate his or her dreams, raise hopes and spirits, and get the organization out of its current situation. A leader must have the ability to create and articulate a realistic and credible vision that can move his or her followers to achieve the organization's goals.

Being a Lifelong Learner

There are many in the younger generations who decide to join the family firm as the fastest way to find a job, particularly in the weak economic situation. The family business leader often easily accepts them, citing family relations as the reason. However, if this family member lacks the competence, lacks the willingness to keep learning, and lacks the ability to cooperate with other people, then he will get into trouble sooner or later. If he cannot contribute to the company, the employees will no longer respect him. His position will weaken and no longer be safe because it is in the employees' best interest to make the company thrive so that their source of income is always guaranteed. A good company cannot recruit and retain incompetent employees, regardless of their background. Charles Saerang from Nyonya Maneer Indonesia, in one seminar, said, "It is better to let some of the less competent family members go than to put thousands of committed employees at risk."

Teresita Sy-Coson once said that being Henry Sy's daughter meant she had to work harder and smarter, to battle the preconception that she had inherited the position. She explains, "You have to really prove yourself to get respect. It's not a matter of sitting on a position and saying, 'This is what we will do.' You have to read a lot, understand what is going on, and work as a team."

Ciputra realizes the importance of qualified employees. According to him, the second-generation family member wanting to join the family business must be qualified, must behave professionally, and must comply with the rules. Otherwise, he or she will be asked to work in another company or be a commissioner. If an unqualified employee is recruited, the company will be at risk.

Chapter 6

The Role of the Wife in Overseas Chinese Family Businesses

Traditionally, in a Chinese family business founded by a male, the role of the wife is often invisible to the public. Nevertheless, wives' contribution to the success of family businesses cannot be ignored. They generally are greatly respected and admired by their husband and children. They instill a sense of purpose, responsibility, and community in family members, as well as promote cooperation and spiritual values and provide unconditional support. They also help their husband pass on moral values to the children.

One example is Lee Kim Hua. She is the matriarch of Genting Group, a conglomerate from Malaysia that specializes in tourism, resorts, gaming, plantations, power generation, oil, and gas. Lee Kim Hua is the widow of the late Lim Goh Tong, the founder of Genting Group, who died in 2007 at the age of 89. They have six children and 19 grandchildren. The six children are Lim Siew Lay, Siew Lian, Siew Kim, Tee Keong, Kok Thay, and Chee Wah. Lim Goh Tong himself was known to be a very hard-working man and visionary and his wife has been a tower of strength, supporting him throughout the years. Lee Kim Hua did not interfere in the running of Genting when it was under her late husband; she also leaves the operations to her son today, whom she believes knows best. Genting Group was founded in 1965. Currently, it employs over 58,000 people globally. It has been voted Malaysia's leading corporation and one of Asia's best managed multinationals. The Genting Group is the founder of Star Cruises, the third largest cruise liner company in the world and largest cruise liner in Asia. An announcement was made on June 22, 2011, that Genting would become the new principal partner of English Premier League Club Aston Villa. The deal is to run initially for two seasons from July 2011 to July 2013.

Lee Kim Hua is the richest woman in Malaysia, but she is still known as a humble woman and tries to stay away from the limelight as much as she can. When Lim Goh Tong passed away, he left his fortune to his wife and family members, and the company is now run by his second son, Lim Kok Thay. Lim Goh Tong transferred the chairman-ship of the Genting Group to his son in December 2003.

In the Gokongweis, Elizabeth Yu Gokongwei has passed humility and moral values to her children. All of her children are obedient, hardworking, and humble. Elizabeth Yu Gokongwei is the wife of John Gokongwei, the founder of JG Summit. Lance Gokongwei described his mother as a kindhearted, warm, and very true person. She is the type of person everyone follows not because they fear her, but because they want to make her happy and not disappoint her. John and Elizabeth Yu Gokongwei have six children, namely Lance Gokongwei, Lisa Gokongwei-Cheng, Robina Gokongwei-Pe, Faith Gokongwei-Lim, Marcia Gokongwei-Sy, and Hope Gogkongwei-Tang. They hold var-ious positions in the Gokongwei Group.

Felicidad Tan Sy, the humble and deeply religious wife of SM Group founder Henry Sy, Sr., is said to be the reason SM Malls hold Catholic masses every Sunday. According to her husband, his wife devotes almost all her time and money to the Catholic Church. She is the most devout among his family members.

When Panda Inn first opened in 1973, customers were scarce. Following Chinese superstition, the wife of Master Chef Ming Tsai Cherng, who is also Andrew Cherng's mother, went outside and sprinkled salt on the sidewalk to remove any negative energy that might be keeping customers away. Today, there are over a thousand Panda Express fast-food restaurants in malls, airports, shopping centers, and other prime locations. Regardless of whether we believe in such superstition or not, this story shows the wife's support for her husband's business.

Nevertheless, nowadays the role of the wife in many Chinese family businesses has evolved beyond just moral support. Instead, wives actively participate in developing the business. They are involved in more business activities.

Wife as the Balance of the Husband

At the beginning, overseas Chinese family businesses were set up by male entrepreneurs, individually or with their male relatives. Subsequent generations see husband and wife working together. The wife typically works in specific areas, such as human resources, finance, and accounting. Her good financial investment, professional, technical, and administrative skills are often critical to the survival of the family business. Her ideas and actions often have impact on the company's growth. The wife sometimes pulls back after the business has been developed, and then focuses on helping the family business develop and diversify into new areas of opportunity. The wife also mentors the children and encourages them to decide to choose the family business as a career option. They help children to understand the importance of the business to the family.

Today, while keeping their traditional roles and function, the wives in many Chinese family businesses are involved more actively in the company. Many of them have a better educational background, have strong entrepreneurial skills, and take the formal leadership role with greater independence and autonomy. Another new role includes introducing work—life balance and greater involvement in the local community, while the husband focuses on marketing and production activities.

Sinflora, one of Singapore's largest wholesalers of fresh-cut flowers and plants, is one example of how a wife can contribute to the success of a family business. Occupying a land area of 100,000 square feet at 1 Seletar West Farmway 1, Sinflora is the single largest garden center in Singapore. The company was established in 1979 by Bernard Loo and his wife, Charlotte Lee, both now in their 50s. Mr. Loo's father ran a successful business supplying flowers and plants to florists, but when he wanted to strike out on his own he decided to sell artificial flowers instead. "He did not want to clash with his father's fresh flower business, so we started supplying artificial flowers to florists in Singapore and Malaysia," recalls Mrs. Lee.

However, as quoted from the *Straits Times* (2009), Mrs. Lee's involvement in the family business certainly was not part of the game plan when she married Mr. Loo. She was an air stewardess for about six and a half years before joining her husband at Sinflora. "At first I didn't want to help him and neither did I want to get into the family business, but I just went with the flow and this was how things turned out," Mrs. Lee said. Currently, she is the firm's executive director. She remains optimistic about business prospects, despite the economic situation. "I don't think the plant business will be affected by the economy too much because firstly, how much can a plant cost?" she said. She says her eldest daughter, who is now at university, and her two younger sons have all shown a keen interest in the family business. However, it hasn't been decided who will take over the business.

Another example is Weili Dai. She is co-founder and former chief operating officer of Marvell Technology Group Ltd. We can say that Dai, the mother of two children, is one of the most successful businesswomen in the world today. She has succeeded in transforming Marvell, which was started in 1995, into one of the most reputable semiconductor companies in the world. For Dai, having a good and continuous relationship with customers is very important. Other characteristics that must not be compromised are professionalism, honesty, and integrity. Thanks to her significant contribution, Marvell has signed many profitable strategic partnerships. She also encourages the spread of technology to developing countries to improve the well-being of societies there, as well as to increase the involvement of women in science and technology. *Newsweek* named Dai one of the "150 Women Who Shake the World" for her work in promoting science and technology. Since Marvell was established, Dai has held top positions such as chief operating officer, executive vice president, general manager of the Communications Business Group, director, and corporate secretary of the board.

Dai also plays an active role in charitable activities. For example, she leads Marvell in a partnership with the One Laptop per Child program (OLPC). She also became a board member of Give2Asia, an organization that helps the victims of disasters. University of California, Berkeley, has built Sutardja Dai Hall in recognition of her contribution, along with her husband Sehat Sutardja, CEO of Marvell, and Pantas Sutardja, CTO of Marvell. Sutardja Dai Hall is home to the Center for Information Technology Research in the Interest of Society (CITRIS).

Katherine Tan, the wife of Andrew Tan from Alliance Global Group Inc., Philippines, is the treasurer and sits on the board of his company. In one interview, Andrew said that when he married, his wife became the most influential person in his life. Today, they talk about business almost every day, especially when he has to make important decisions.

Wife as Complement and Driver

Complementary means forming and serving as a complement. A *complement* itself is something that completes or makes perfect. In the context of a family business, its success depends on its ability to make the business thrive while at the same time being able to maintain the family harmony for generations.

In many Chinese family businesses, a wife can be a complement to her husband. While the husband focuses his attention on the success of the business, the wife focuses hers on keeping the family together so that all of the members can work harmoniously.

Although not all the wives of Chinese family founders or leaders are actively involved in the business, their important role in keeping the family and business together is not in doubt. The wives, as suggested by Poza (2008), often see themselves as the glue that keeps everyone united through the challenges that families who work together commonly face. They act as healers and mediators for their family. They also often take responsibility for family initiatives, such as creating a family council, hosting family gatherings, and planning family vacations and multi-generational celebrations.

In the business context, a *driver* is an aspect that effects a change on another aspect of the business. A driver is most commonly a factor that contributes to the growth of a particular business. In a family business, the wife can also be a driver to the company's growth. The wife in many Chinese family businesses is the initiator of professionalism and greater delegation so that the company will no longer be too dependent on the founder or senior leader.

Wife as the Secretary

A *secretary* is a person whose work consists of supporting management, including executives and using a variety of project management, communication, and organizational skills. A secretary personally helps top executives in an organization. In his or her work, a secretary can help multiple employees. A secretary can also be someone in a society or an organization whose job includes sending and receiving letters, acknowledging new people, and coordinating organization events.

A secretary has many administrative duties. Traditionally, these duties were mostly related to correspondence, such as typing letters, maintaining files of paper documents, and so on. The advent of word processing has significantly reduced the time that such duties require, with the result that many new tasks have come under the range of the secretary. These might include managing budgets, doing bookkeeping, and making travel arrangements. Secretaries might manage all of the administrative details of running a high-level conference or arrange the catering for a typical lunch meeting. Often executives will ask their secretary to take the minutes at meetings and prepare meeting documents for review.

In many Chinese family businesses, the wife is a reliable secretary to her husband, and often business operation activities cannot run smoothly without her. For the husband, his wife's role as secretary is so important that there was one owner who said that his wife could not be fired since she is "one in a million." In other words, his wife's role as secretary is irreplaceable.

Wife as the Most Important Figure Following Her Husband's Death

Following the death of her husband, the wife, who is also a mother, becomes the central figure not just in the family but in the business as well. Her role in keeping the family and business together is even more important following her husband's death. She ensures that after their father's death, the children will not be involved in a bitter conflict that could ruin the family and the business. However, this does not necessarily mean that she holds the highest formal position in the company.

One example of a wife who still has strong influence even after her husband's death is Beatrice Campos. She is the widow of Jose Yao Campos, who co-founded United Laboratories (Unilab) along with Mariano Tan. Jose Yao Campos died in May 2006. Currently, Beatrice Campos ranks number 19 in *Forbes Asia*'s 40 Richest Filipinos. She also controls Singapore-listed Del Monte Pacific, run by son Joselito. Unilab is the biggest pharmaceutical company in the Philippines. Established in 1945, it was the first among local companies to go into industrial-scale pharmaceutical manufacturing. By 1959, it had a robust nationwide distribution and sales network. Its portfolio includes some of the biggest prescription and consumer healthcare brands in the country. The company has also consistently maintained a 20 percent market share, with many of its brands becoming the most trusted household names and leading in their therapeutic categories. Today, Unilab has affiliates in 10 countries in the Asia-Pacific region.

In the Chinese tradition, it is the eldest son who usually takes over control of the family business. However, he also has the primary responsibility for the welfare of his mother after his father's death. This is in accordance with the teaching of filial piety. He often defers to her wishes and always treats her with respect. This shows how a wife, who is also a mother, is the most important person after her husband's death.

In 2008, Lim Kok Thay from Genting Group was presented with a professorship by Xiamen University of China. The news was accompanied by the announcement of an HKD 6 million donation from Star Cruise to the Tourism Department of the University for a building to be named after Lim Goh Tong, the late founder of the group. The donation and appointment ceremonies were held at Xiamen University. To show great respect for the occasion, Lim Kok Thay traveled with his mother, Lee Kim Hua, and his brother, Lim Chee Wah, from Malaysia to China to present the donation to President Zhu Chong-Shi, who received it on behalf of the university.

The Role of a Wife: A Breaker or a Binder?

Every family has its own rules regarding money, loyalty, togetherness, image, conflict, and roles, although these rules are seldom written. *Role* consists of a set of behaviors, rights, and obligations that should be performed. Role includes expectations regarding how family members should behave themselves. Each role is set by a rule. Rules about roles give family members clues regarding how they should live their life.

In a family business, rules about roles are often transferred from the family life to the business life. In family life, we find the wife (and mother) who tries to take care of everything, including business matters. She feels that if she does not do this, everything will be out of order. Therefore, although without a formal position, the wife might have great access to the business resources, particularly the financial ones. If not dealt with carefully, this could have a negative impact on the business. We can say that in such situations, the wife might play the role of a breaker who can potentially break the business. To overcome this situation, the role of the wife in a family business should be defined more clearly, including the ways in which she can make positive contributions to the business. This can be reached through compromise and negotiation between husband, wife, and children.

In a family business, the wife is not just the spouse of her husband. Instead, she is also the mother of their children. These children are expected to take over control of the business someday in the future. As a mother, she is expected to exert great influence in educating her children and to help her husband to prepare the children so that they are ready to take control of the business. She does that using her motherly touch. She also is expected to instill the sense of togetherness and pride in her children so that they are ready to give their best for the family and for the business. By educating the children well and by instilling the sense of togetherness and pride, a wife/mother plays her role as a binder, the one who unites her family so that the purposes of the family and the business can be accomplished.

Regarding the wife's role in educating the children, again we take a look at Beatrice Campos. Her youngest son, Jeffrey Y.D. Campos, is now the chairman of the real estate firm Greenfield Development Corporation. Jeffrey attributes his family's strategy of investing in numerous realty properties, from Metro Manila to sprawling landholdings in Santa Rosa, Laguna, to his mother.

Chapter 7

Leadership Styles of Overseas Chinese Family Businesses

L eadership style refers to the behavior of a leader based on his or her personality, philosophy, and background. There are some leadership styles that can be applied by leaders of any organization, including leaders of Chinese family businesses.

Suitable leadership style depends on the situation faced by the leader. An autocratic leadership style may be most effective when there is a time limit to decide something or when leaders have more knowledge, skill, resources, and experience compared to their followers. However, in an organization where employees have high motivations and various skills, a more democratic leadership style should be applied. A leader must choose a leadership style which is the most effective in helping the organization achieve its goal, while at the same time accommodating the employees' interests and aspirations. So, we can say that there are no right or wrong leadership styles.

From Dictatorship to Democracy

In the early years, when the business had just been established, Chinese family business founders, without a doubt, adopted an autocratic or authoritarian leadership style. In authoritarian leadership, a leader has an absolute and unchallenged power, controls his or her followers tightly, and asks his or her followers to obey without asking any questions. Authoritarian leadership is one of the three dimensions of paternalistic leadership, according to Cheng and Lim (2012). The other dimension is benevolent and moral leadership. Benevolent leadership means that the leader has individual, overall, and permanent concern for subordinates. And moral leadership requires a leader to display a high level of personal integrity or accomplishments to win the respect and admiration of subordinates.

Under the autocratic leadership style, all decision-making powers are centralized in the leaders, based on their intuition and experience. In a Chinese family business context, it is the founder who has the absolute power. He is the single dominant owner, manager, entrepreneur, founder, and father figure. Autocratic leaders keep strict, close control over followers by keeping a close regulation on policies and procedures given to followers. They believe that direct supervision is the key if an organization wants to achieve success. Because they fear that followers may be unproductive, authoritarian leaders keep close supervision and feel this is necessary in order for anything to be done. Effective supervision is often provided through detailed orders and instructions.

In an authoritarian leadership style, the leader does not consult employees. He does not take suggestions or initiatives from subordinates into consideration. He sometimes does not even trust his employees. Employees are expected to obey orders without asking for any explanations. They are in no position to challenge the leader's authority directly. Clear differentiation exists between the leader and their subordinates.

In an authoritarian leadership style, in order to maintain his power, the family business owner controls the flow of information. He transmits information only in small amounts to his subordinates so that they become dependent and thus unable to outperform him. The amount of information given to a specific subordinate depends on the degree of trust that the leader has for that individual. Without the control of information, the subordinates frequently have to ask the leader for instructions.

Autocratic management has been successful as it provides strong motivation to the subordinates. The authoritarian leadership style enables quick decision-making, as only one person decides for the whole group or organization. Other characteristics of authoritarian leadership style include setting goals individually, engaging primarily in one way, adopting downward communication, and controlling discussions with followers (Martindale, 2011).

Authoritarian leadership is effective when there are new or untrained employees who need to know which task to perform or which procedures to follow, when new or untrained employees need supervision with detailed orders and instructions, when some employees do not respond to any leadership style and really challenge the authority of their manager, and when there are high volumes of production needed and only limited time to make a decision.

An authoritarian leadership style is usually adopted by a dictator. A dictator is a ruler who assumes sole and absolute power. Again, this kind of person is common within Chinese family business founders. In a dictatorship, an organization is ruled by individuals who are often unrestricted by rules, structure, and system.

Nevertheless, as the company grows and more people with different characteristics join the business, the authoritarian style of leadership can no longer be maintained since it could create resentment, fear, and tension, which could lead to lower employee morale, higher absentees and turnover, and work stoppage. Greater participation must be promoted since more employees want their opinion to be heard.

Therefore, leaders must change their leadership style. A style called *laissez-faire* leadership is encouraged. In this style, leaders let their followers decide freely on how to do their job. In other words, followers are given more freedom. However, this does not mean leaders do not support and guide their followers, although leaders do not participate directly in making decisions, unless the followers ask them to do so. The laissez-faire leader also provides his or her followers with necessary resources so that they can do their job smoothly. Laissez-faire leadership is beneficial when followers have high skills, knowledge, education, and experience; love and feel proud about their job; have a strong desire to succeed; and can be trusted. However, the laissez-faire leadership style should not be used when followers do not feel safe when their leaders are not around, when leaders cannot make suggestions regularly, and when followers do not understand their responsibilities. If a Chinese family business leader wants to adopt this style, he or she needs to instill a sense of pride in both the family members and the non-family employees.

The democratic style of leadership can be promoted if a company wants to create equality. In democratic-style leadership, a leader gives his or her followers all available information that could affect their work on a regular basis. He or she also allows the followers to make decisions. In this style, discussion, debate, and exchange of ideas is common. Members' involvement is appreciated. The democratic style encompasses the notion that everyone should play a part in the group's decisions. Nevertheless, guidance and control are still needed.

Because freedom to express any thoughts and ideas is guaranteed, democratic-style leadership will stimulate fresh ideas and solutions. It also encourages employees to make self-evaluations regarding their performance, with the help of the leader. The leader also lets the employees decide their own goals, as well as encourages and recognizes self-development and achievements.

Although it seems ideal, this kind of leadership style is not always suitable. It must not be used when roles are not clearly defined and there is a time limit, because it will create problems in communication and hinder project completion. It must also not be used when mistakes and failure will cost the company a huge loss (not just financially), and when safety and security are at risk. In a situation when employees have high skills and knowledge and are ready to share them, and when there is enough time for all to participate, then democratic-style leadership will be effective.

If the authoritarian leadership style can no longer be sustained, then which leadership style would a Chinese family business adopt? Most Chinese family businesses want the family to keep the control in their hands. Nevertheless, many of them no longer hesitate to give employees more freedom to make decisions regarding their work, while at the same time the founder or senior family member provides guidance and support. Some have even made further steps by engaging their employees in discussion, debate, and sharing of ideas regarding the latest business issues. This step is often promoted by the younger generations in Chinese family businesses, many of whom graduated from western universities in the United States, UK, Australia, and other European countries. This in turn often creates fresh ideas and solutions. They also develop plans to help employees evaluate their own performance, allow employees to establish goals, encourage employees to grow on the job and be promoted, and recognize and encourage achievement. By doing this, these Chinese family businesses have actually adopted a democratic leadership style.

One example is Lance Gokongwei from JG Summit, Philippines. Currently, he serves as president and CEO of Cebu Air, Inc., operating as Cebu Pacific Air. Cebu Pacific Air is the subsidiary of JG Summit Holdings. The airline was established on August 26, 1988, and started operations on March 8, 1996. It initially started with 24 domestic flights daily among Metro Manila, Metro Cebu, and Metro Davao. By the end of 2001, its operations had grown to about 80 daily flights to 18 domestic destinations.

Cebu Pacific Air is currently the country's leading domestic carrier, serving the most domestic destinations with the largest number of flights and routes and equipped with the youngest fleet. The company has 1,182 employees. In October 2010, the airline completed an IPO of

30.4 percent of its outstanding shares. Cebu Pacific carried more than 10 million passengers in 2010.

In the 2000s, Cebu Pacific was granted rights to operate international flights in the region, including Malaysia, Indonesia, Singapore, Thailand, South Korea, Hong Kong, and Guam. International flights were launched on November 22, 2001, with twice-daily service to Hong Kong. On March 1, 2002, it commenced thrice-weekly flights to Seoul. The airlines launched its direct flight from Cebu to Singapore on October 23, 2006, the first low-cost airline to serve the Cebu-Singapore-Cebu sector, and in direct competition with Singapore Airlines' subsidiary, SilkAir. CEB is now the only Philippines carrier serving the Cebu-Singapore-Cebu route after Philippines Airlines (PAL) terminated its direct service. Recently, Cebu Pacific has been named the 2012 Low-Cost Carrier of the Year. Its CEO, Lance Gokongwei, has been named the Low-Cost Carrier CEO of the Year during the prestigious Budgies & Travel Awards of 2012.

Aside from his job as president and CEO of Cebu Pacific Air, Lance Gokongwei holds key positions in JG Summit Holdings. Lance Gokongwei attributes the success of Cebu Pacific Air to its affordable rates, excellent service, reliability, on-time performance, and commitment to safety. He has a pool of honest, hardworking, and dedicated people committed to providing customer satisfaction. His employees work as a team and he rewards them. Lance Gokongwei also encourages employees to talk directly to management and asks for their suggestions on how to improve the business. It is his leadership style that makes his company thrive in the airline industry.

Cebu Pacific Air probably reflects Lance Gokongwei's personality and leadership style the best. His leadership style is distinguished as "more operational, more focused, and more consensual." He is humble and prudent, but he is ambitious. The Cebu Pacific Air offices and airline environment are casual, friendly, practical, no-frills, no-nonsense, and fun. Its in-flight magazine is called *Smile* and its brochures and websites are dotted with local puns. CEB's casual uniform of walking shorts and a polo shirt or a sleek knit suit sets the tone for a "fun flight" as the company calls it. Lance Gokongwei rarely wears a suit or tie, and dresses down at the office in rolled-up shirtsleeve and chinos, or in company-issued polo shirts.

Another example is Eu Yan Sang. Eu Yan Sang hired K.F. Tan as a group controller; he then became chief financial officer of Eu Yan Sang. Currently, he serves as the company's chief operating officer. When he was hired as group controller, Eu Yan Sang was looking for a finance executive who could work well with operations and eventually participate in strategic discussions. After beginning his career in finance, Tan served as general manager for NatSteel Chemicals in Singapore, and as managing director for Nextec, a U.S. fabric company. Life at this company closely resembled the multinationals where Tan had worked previously. "This is a very professionally managed company," he says. "Corporate decisions are made by consensus. Richard Eu, the chief executive officer of Eu Yan Sang, doesn't come and say 'Hey, K.F., I want this to be done.' We freely share our views and come to an agreement."

Yearning for a Patriarch

As many Chinese family businesses start to adopt a more democratic style of leadership—marked by family members' collective leadership and greater participation from non-family employees—they nevertheless always yearn for someone who can act as a patriarch or matriarch, even when the founder or senior leader is no longer with the company. As Raphael Amit, the Wharton professor of entrepreneurship who studies family businesses, once said, "With succession in family businesses, it's not just a question of who will head the business but who will be the new patriarch of the family." *Patriarch* is a man who is the father or the founder, while *matriarch* is a woman who rules or dominates a family, group, or state.

In this family business context, patriarch (or matriarch) refers to someone who is considered older, has many experiences, is considered wise, and is respected by all family members. The person could be anyone. The patriarch can give advice and provide guidance regarding the business and family so that both of them will remain intact. He also provides emotional support, keeps communication open, protects family tradition and values, and makes sure that the family gets together to socialize and have fun. Most importantly, this patriarch would act as a mediator should there be any disagreement, fight, or conflict among leaders. Usually, if there are multiple leaders in an organization, there is a greater possibility that these leaders would fight for recognition. Chinese family businesses are no exception, particularly those that do not strictly adhere to Confucian values.

Consider what happened with Bukit Kiara Properties (BKP), a leading Malaysian real estate development firm. Since its inception in 2000, BKP has been led by the experienced and renowned Alan Tong Kok Mau and his son, N.K. Tong. In 1990, they turned acres of rubber estate land near the fringe of Sri Hartamas in Kuala Lumpur into one of the country's most exclusive and premium residential addresses, now known as Mont'Kiara. This unique name of Mont'Kiara is now associated with exclusivity that is attributed to Alan and N.K. Tong. Today, with over 1,000 customers, BKP has four subsidiaries, namely Bukit Kiara Builders (BKB), Civil Contractor; Bukit Kiara Interiors (BKI), Interiors Contractor; Bukit Kiara Property Services (BKPS), Property Management; and Tunas Landscape, Landscape Contractor. BKP, BKB, BKI, and BKPS are all ISO 9001:2008 certified companies. The Al Batha Group, one of the largest conglomerates in the United Arab Emirates, entered into a 40:60 joint venture with the Bukit Kiara Group in October 2008. With the joint venture, the group is now known as Al Batha Bukit Kiara Holdings, but the BKP brand name will continue to be used.

BKP won the Malaysian Business Ethics Excellence Award three times in a row, in 2006, 2008, and 2010. The Malaysian Business Ethics Excellence Award is held every two years. It recognizes companies practicing exemplary business ethics guided by their respective Code of Ethics. In addition, BKP became the first property development company to win the Best Overall Small and Medium Business Award in December 2005. In November 2006, BKP won the Product Innovation Excellence Award from the Small and Medium Industries Association of Malaysia.

On one occasion, N.K. Tong, who currently serves as the managing director of BKP, suggested that it was his aunt who always brought the family together. "When she picks up the phone, everyone comes running," says Tong. Her effectiveness at bringing people together was essential in the late 1990s, when Tong and his father, Alan Tong Kok Mau, sold one family business and started Bukit Kiara. "My dad asked her to find out which family members wanted to join us, and over a single weekend she raised a fair sum of money from over 20 [of them]."

Although leaders of Chinese family businesses always need a patriarch to help them make the business thrive and maintain a harmonious relationship among family members, they do not want this patriarch to boss them around. In other words, the leaders do not accept a patriarch who gives orders in an arrogant or domineering manner.

Chapter 8

The Importance of Social Organization in Chinese Family Businesses

In this context, social organization refers to a group of overseas Chinese businessmen who gather to perform activities for certain social and political objectives for organizing blood drives and promoting political agendas for eliminating discrimination against ethnic Chinese and gaining stronger political influence.

Evolution of the Bamboo Network

The bamboo network is a network of close-knit Chinese entrepreneurs with large corporate empires in Southeast Asia. It consists of conglomerates in the Southeast Asia region that started as small family businesses run by overseas Chinese families. Later, the bamboo network made great contributions in spurring economic growth in Southeast Asian countries such as Indonesia, Malaysia, Thailand, the Philippines, and Singapore. The founders of these conglomerates typically started with little wealth. They built their family enterprises from scratch and then worked, saved, and reinvested. One exception might be Robert Kuok. He was born to a successful rice, flour, and sugar trader.

The businesses are managed by the founder and his family: sons, brothers, nephews, in-laws, and also daughters and nieces. This provides loyalty, flexibility, fast decision-making, and low overhead cost. The businesses are run with strong Confucian values. "To live is to love others, to honor one's parents, to do what is right instead of doing what is to advantage, to practice reciprocity, and to rule by moral example instead of by force and violence." This famous Confucius quote is useful in showing how Confucianism strongly affects business structure and the bamboo network.

With social organization, the bamboo network can increase its presence globally. Typically, a successful family will own many businesses spread over a number of countries. For example, Robert Kuok has many investments in many countries throughout Asia, including Singapore, the Philippines, Thailand, Mainland China, and Indonesia, as well as in Australia and Fiji. Businesses in China include ten bottling companies for Coca-Cola and ownership of the Beijing World Trade Center. Another example is Bangkok Bank, founded by Chin Sophonpanich. Its branch network includes over 1,000 branches within Thailand, with 26 international branches or representative offices in 13 economies, spanning ASEAN and other major economic countries, including wholly owned subsidiaries in Malaysia and China. Bangkok Bank also owns branches in London and New York to complement its extensive network in Southeast Asia. It is Thailand's largest bank, and the seventh largest regional bank in Southeast Asia. The bank is a publicly listed company and among the top five companies in terms of size listed on the Stock Exchange of Thailand (SET). Bangkok Bank has a full range of business, investment banking, and personal banking services. It is one of the most active global traders of Thai baht and Thai baht–denominated bonds. The bank trades in all major currencies as well as a large number of regional currencies. Other services include same-day transactions in import and export bills, inward and outward remittances, swaps, options and forward contracts, and trading in the primary and secondary markets for government bonds and corporate debentures. Bangkok Bank currently has the largest overseas branch network of any Thai bank in 13 economies, including wholly owned subsidiaries in Malaysia and China and one representative office in Myanmar.

Control of the business is generally passed from generation to generation, and since for the most part the receivers of the business have already had an active managerial role, the transitions tend to be quite smooth. One of Robert Kuok's sons, Kuok Khoon Ean, now handles most of the day-to-day operations of his father's businesses. In Indonesia, Sudono Salim turned over the management of Salim Group to his son, Anthony Salim, in 1992.

Most, if not all, managerial positions within a company in the bamboo network will be filled by family members. Other strategic posts are usually reserved for close relatives and for those who have worked for the family for long periods of time. This means that there is a significant amount of trust at the top of the company. It also means that the top business executives are more likely to sit and have a conversation, which is often informal, to plan company strategy or discuss issues rather than handing each other paperwork or arranging formal meetings. Discussions with friends and family are more dominant. According to a source, as reported by *AsiaViews* (2004) family members and employees in Kuok Group communicate with each other in a more relaxed manner. Memos are often used to send messages. Employees often use initials to mention someone's name, like R.K. for Robert Kuok, B.K. for Beau Kuok, and C.K. for Chye Kuok. Top executives usually meet every year in Hong Kong. But again, the atmosphere is relaxed and informal as if it is a vacation time. However, since family members' influence is dominant, even non-family trusted persons have to consult with the family before deciding on strategic matters.

Kinship, dialect, and origin are the foundation for mutual trust in business transactions in the network. Common values in the bamboo network include hard work, meticulousness, faithfulness, and trust of families and friends. Top executives keep the important information secret.

In the company, leaders will not let information flow freely. Trust will determine the amount and quality of information and knowledge given to followers, which is different for every person. The more someone is trusted, the more information will be given, and vice versa.

Members of the bamboo network prefer doing business with other members within the network. The bamboo network is also the main source of information. Members usually do not use market research techniques to find information about markets and customers.

The bureaucracy in the bamboo network is simple. At the same time, the personal relationships the management teams have with each other are very strong. The bamboo network has a unique ability when dealing with government regulations and restrictions because of its ability to shift money, people, and resources from one country to another (Weidenbaum, 1998).

Trust is one of the most important factors in the bamboo network, and only employees who have worked with their employer for a long time will hold higher positions than family members. A professional manager in Kuok Group revealed that for Robert Kuok, faithfulness from professionals is extremely important. These faithful professionals, most of whom are Kuok's good friends, will have a chance to decide important issues. Because the leader of the company is generally the head of the family, he has the power in the business sense and in the social sense, which can be effective in maintaining control, since he will have more experience than his children and because they have the responsibility to respect him in all spheres of life.

As the family conglomerates have grown, they have served as incubators for the future management of related enterprises. Robert Kuok from Malaysia is one example. One of the factors that determine the Kuok Group's success is the close connection of the Kuoks with the leading families of Asia. They include Sudono Salim of Indonesia and Chin Sophonpanich of Thailand. The partnership between the Sophonpanichs and the Kuoks extends even to the Shangri-La in Bangkok. Chin Sophonanich's son, Chatri Sophonpanich, is a joint-venture partner in the city's leading luxury hotel. Salim is also Kuok's close associate. Salim once said that Kuok had succeeded in obtaining licenses issued by the Indonesian Bureau of Logistics to supply sugar in Indonesia through his help in the 1970s.

The typical bamboo network enterprise has a low profile position or attitude and is characterized by the deliberate avoidance of prominence or publicity. People like Robert Kuok and Sudono Salim have such characteristics. Kuok, for example, is media-shy. He once said, "Tall trees experience strong winds." Another example is Jose Yao Campos, the founder of United Laboratories (Unilab). He was so low profile that a *Who's-Who* book on business VIPs once wrongly used the photo of a Philippine stockbroker as the picture of the Unilab founder. Almost no photos of Campos have been published during his legendary career.

The enterprises serve as middlemen, making components for someone else. The owners know the key government officials of the countries in which they operate and they are great dealmakers. Yet they do not produce or market any major consumer product and therefore have little experience in managing large manufacturing operations. Talking about great dealmakers, academician Dr. Edmund Terence Gomez from the University of Malaya, Malaysia, once said that Robert Kuok is one of the best dealmakers. He has been able to capitalize on opportunities, and synergism among his group of companies further enhances his networking success. These linkages provide the basis for Kuok's expansion in Asia. According to a top lieutenant, Kuok is the dealmaker of the Group. "He would use this networking for business expansion and patronage while the professional managers would work out the details of these deals," the lieutenant said.

The bamboo network has many advantages, such as no conflicting values, since the owners also serve as controlling managers. The faster decision making is important so that the leaders can concentrate their time and resources on business activities that add value and a high level of interaction and lead discussions that could strengthen personal relationships. Nevertheless, bamboo networks also have some disadvantages, such as low use of technology in nature since businesses in the bamboo network were started as very small, family-run operations. Low technology can be practiced and fabricated with minimum capital investments, by an individual or small group of individuals. In low technology, the knowledge of the practice can be completely understood by a single individual. It is also relatively free from specialization. This makes the barrier to enter the industry low.

The role of the bamboo network has been extended. It does not merely function as a means to grow the businesses of the network. Its presence is also aimed at maintaining Chinese culture and maintaining the needs of the members and their offspring to continue their legacy and inheritance. For example, in Indonesia there are some organizations founded by those of Chinese descent. They are founded by Chinese senior businesspersons who already have more time and money. Every member of such an organization is expected to be ready to give something in return for the help they have received.

As observed in other cultures, the societal community became more formal as their businesses grew. The community became an important place for businessmen to get to know each other and exchange information, and for some even to become influential in politics. This idea is similar to the Jewish community establishing the Jewish Community Center (JCC). The JCC is a general recreational, social, and fraternal organization serving the Jewish community in a number of cities. JCCs promote Jewish culture and heritage through holiday celebrations, Israel-related programming, and Jewish education; however, they are open to everyone in the community. The JCC Association is the continental umbrella organization for the Jewish Community Center movement, which includes more than 350 JCCs and campsites in the United States and Canada, in addition to 180 local JCCs in the former Soviet Union, 70 in Latin America, 50 in Europe, and close to 500 smaller centers in Israel.

The bamboo network also resembles the Greek Diaspora, the community of Greek people living outside the traditional Greek homelands. Members of the diaspora can be identified as those who migrated, or whose ancestors migrated, from their Greek homelands. Today, the important centers of the Greek Diaspora are New York, Chicago, Boston, London, Melbourne, Sydney, Montreal, and Toronto. The Greek Diaspora is very active as a lobby defending Greek interests. Integration, intermarriage, and loss of the Greek language also influence the definition and self-definition of Greeks of the diaspora. The goal of this organization is "to bring together the diaspora of Greeks creating a global network aimed at planning and materializing programs for the benefit of the Omogeneia to be subsequently conveyed to the Greek state thus fulfilling its role as an advisory and consultative body."

Founder's Activities for Retirement

In many literatures about family business, it is often suggested that the psychological and financial security of the founder should be addressed before he is ready to hand over the power to the younger generation. However, in many Chinese family businesses, the psychological and financial security of the founder after his retirement is seldom a problem. Although the founder has formally announced his retirement to the public and the successor has been named, in reality he still has strong influence within the company and his family. As a result, the retirement of the founder is rarely realized by either family members or employees, or this fact is seldom even revealed to the public.

One example is Robert Kuok, the "sugar king." The story was revealed in 2004 by *AsiaViews* magazine. At that time it was discovered that Kuok had emerged from semiretirement in 2003 following the death of his most trusted lieutenant and nephew-in-law, Richard Liu Tai Fung. Kuok and his family did not confirm this issue since they are media shy. However, Chye, head of the Group's Malaysia operations and chairman of Kuok Brothers Sdn Bhd, granted *AsiaViews* an interview. Family friends and former professional managers also spoke, but on condition of anonymity.

Making a comeback at the age of 80 is not easy. Underlying this comeback were rumors that Kuok was getting apprehensive over succession plans at the Group. "His main concern appears to be how to avoid a family squabble," a family friend revealed. Some say Kuok's active return was to iron out details of succession plans at the Group. Until Richard Liu Tai Fung's sudden death at the KL International Airport in 2003, Kuok was grooming him as heir apparent. Liu was said to be a neutral leader, balancing the interests of both Kuok's children and those of his brother, Philip Kuok Hock Khee (Philip died on December 12, 2003. He had two sons and two daughters). Nevertheless, not all agreed with this opinion. Albert Saychuan Cheok, who at that time was the chairman of Bangkok Bank, argued that Robert Kuok had always been there and "would always continue to be there, both for the family and the group." For Chye, the most important thing in Robert Kuok's mind is the group's quest for new business opportunities that would add synergy to the existing operations. Regardless of which story is true, in Chinese family businesses the founder often still provides guidance for the business and the family even after he announces his retirement.

Another example is Vincent Tan from Berjaya, Malaysia. On February 23, 2012, Vincent decided to retire from his position as chairman of Berjaya Corporation Berhad (BCorp). Nevertheless, his son, Robin, revealed that his father will not abandon the company completely. Instead, Vincent will always provide guidance and direction to ensure that the company will have a bright future. After his retirement, Vincent will concentrate on community development and empowerment activities. Vincent, whose wealth is worth US$1.2 billion, according to *Forbes* magazine, handed over business management to his son, Robin.

Vincent himself revealed that although he will no longer be involved in the company's daily activities, he is still the controlling shareholder of Berjaya and his commitment to the company he founded will never change. He can retire comfortably because the company will be run by the right people. He believes in the ability of his sons, Robin and Rayvin, to bring the company into the future, as well as the ability of professional managers working in the company. Nevertheless, he is always ready to provide guidance. He also feels that by stepping down from the top management position in Berjaya, he can focus his time, energy, and mind to be involved more in social activities. Having Robin say that his father would continue to advise and guide at all times and that he still had the interest of the group at heart, it is expected that Vincent Tan will still have great influence in the company.

Serving as an advisor and providing guidance to the company, as well as establishing foundations for social activities, are common things that many Chinese family business founders do after announcing their retirement. However, many of them are involved in social organizations such as civic societies. Such involvement can even be done before retirement, and can be intensified after the founder leaves the business.

This social organization will provide leeway to expand and explore the founder's contribution and influence.

Let us take a look at some Philippine nationals of Chinese ethnicity, known as Chinese Filipinos. Aside from their family businesses, Chinese Filipinos are active in civic organizations related to education, health care, public safety, social welfare, and public charity, in which prominent Chinese family business founders are expected to join. As most Chinese Filipinos are reluctant to participate in politics and government, they have instead turned to civic organizations as their primary means of contributing to the general welfare of the Chinese-Filipino community and to the betterment of Philippine society. Beyond the traditional family and clan associations, Chinese Filipinos tend to be active members of numerous alumni associations holding annual reunions for the benefit of their Chinese-Filipino secondary schools.

Some Chinese-Filipino benefactors have also contributed to the creation of several centers of scholarship in prestigious Philippine universities, including the John Gokongwei School of Management at Ateneo de Manila University, the Yuchengco Center at De La Salle University, and the Ricardo Leong Center for Chinese Studies at Ateneo de Manila.

In the arts and culture, the Bahay Tsinoy and the Yuchengco Museum were established by Chinese Filipinos. Bahay Tsinoy documents the history, lives, and contributions of the Chinese in Philippine life and history. The museum was designed by Eva Penamora in collaboration with the late architect Honrado Fernandez in 1996, and completed and inaugurated in 1999. Kaisa Para Sa Kaunlaran, Inc., is a nonprofit organization co-founded by Teresita Ang-See, who envisioned the project to provide another venue for advocating patriotism to the Philippines and promoting cultural identity and understanding between the local Chinese and Filipino communities. Funding for the land and building structure was advanced by the Angelo King Foundation, which eventually raised monies through generous contributions from different levels of the Filipino-Chinese community, from taipans to average wage-earners.

Alfonso T. Yuchengco, from Yuchengco Group of Companies and Rizal Commercial Banking Corporation, also serves as the chairman of the Board of Trustees of the Mapua Institute of Technology, the top-performing engineering school in the Philippines. He also has been a member of the Board of Advisors of the Columbia Business School, one of the leading business schools in the world. He is a member of the Board of Judges and a Principal Sponsor in the Mother Teresa Awards.

The Yuchengco Museum opened its doors to the public in September 2005. The museum was created to house the art collection of Alfonso and highlight his distinguished career as a businessman, diplomat, collector, philanthropist, and patron of the arts, and advocate for education in the Philippines and beyond. The museum's primary goal is to foster a greater public appreciation of the finest in Filipino and Filipino-Chinese visual arts and creativity.

In addition to his activities in Yayasan Tan Sri Dato' Lee Shin Cheng, Lee Shin Cheng, the founder of the IOI Group from Malaysia, also serves as a board member of Universiti Putra Malaysia, the adviser to the KL and the Selangor Chinese Chamber of Commerce and Industry, a council member of Malaysian Palm Oil Association (MPOA), a member of the Malaysia-China Business Council, and the honorary president of the Association of Eng Choon Societies of Malaysia and the Federation of Hokkien Association of Malaysia. Lee, as well as Robert Kuok, is among the richest persons in Malaysia.

Eka Tjipta Widjaja founded the Eka Tjipta Foundation (ETF), a nonprofit organization, in 2006. The organization aims to improve quality of life and welfare, and foster self-supporting society by providing sustainable contributions through various programs that are economically viable, socially equitable, and environmentally sustainable. The foundation focuses its programs in the education sector and environmental conservation, as well as alternative energy empowerment. The well-being of many societies in Indonesia has been enhanced thanks to the activities of the ETF. For example, the ETF has helped rebuild schools that collapsed because of the 2006 earthquake in Yogyakarta. Through the "Economics for Life" education programs in collaboration with Junior Achievement Indonesia, ETF teaches entrepreneurship and professional business practices to 3,500 high school students in East Java. Scholarships to several high institutions in Indonesia are also provided.

Lee Seng Tee is another example of a Chinese family business leader who is active in social organizations. He is the son of Lee Kong Chian.

Lee makes contributions to enhance the quality of higher education throughout the world. He is particularly interested in providing a high quality reading venue, as well as supporting the acquisition of published resources for some of the most famous libraries in the world, including the Needham Research Institute at the University of Cambridge and the Bodleian Library at the University of Oxford. The Chartered Institute of Library and Information Professionals has awarded him for his contributions and dedication to libraries around the world. Lee is also interested in making contributions in sport by supporting the Chinese Chess Association. Lee Seng Tee Library has been established in Beijing. Tournaments such as the ST Lee Beijing International Open and the Lee Seng Tee Cup have also been held. Lee Seng Tee Public Library in Nan'an City, Fujian Province is another of Lee's contribution to society, particularly in China. He also teaches in several top universities, such as Cambridge and Oxford in the United Kingdom; Columbia University, Harvard University, Stanford University, the Institute for Advanced Studies, and Princeton, in the United States; the University of Sydney in Australia; Victoria University in Wellington, New Zealand; the University of Witwatersrand in South Africa, and the National University of Singapore. Lee Seng Tee also serves as an Honorary Fellow of the British Academy (1999), and Foreign Honorary Member of the American Academy of Arts and Sciences (2001), as well as an Honorary Fellow of Wolfson College, Cambridge, and Oriel College, Oxford. Lee is a Member of the Guild of Cambridge Benefactors.

Chapter 9

Dealing with Risk

isk refers to any negative and/or harmful consequences of an action or something that can happen. A risk consists of probability and severity. Probability is the chance that something negative or harmful can happen, while severity measures how devastating the impact would be if that something happens or if an action is taken. Nevertheless, every individual does not have the same attitude toward risk because it depends on perception. Perception can change from time to time, depending on someone's understanding and experience. Someone who has a bad experience usually tends to avoid risk.

There are some people who are totally uncomfortable with risk; hence they try to avoid it at all costs. In contrast, there are also people who do not fear risk. They are ready to take risks and accept the consequences. For them, dealing with negative consequences creates its own challenges, which they enjoy. In between, there are some persons who are ready to take risks within certain limits, such as time limits.

These kinds of people are ready to take risks but only temporarily. They cannot afford to take risks for a long period of time.

An individual or a group is also different regarding how much risk it is willing to accept before an action is considered necessary to reduce it. This is called risk appetite. The level of risk appetite will depend on the nature of the work undertaken and the objectives pursued. For example, when public safety is critical, risk appetite tends to be low. But for an innovative project, it may be very high, with the acceptance of short-term failure that could pave the way to long-term success. Individuals or organizations have different approaches regarding risk appetite. There are individuals or organizations that avoid risk as their objective. Some are willing to take only minimal risk. As a result, the potential for greater rewards is low. There are also individuals or organizations that are willing to consider all potential options and choose the one most likely to result in successful delivery while also providing an acceptable level of reward and value for money. Individuals or organizations with the highest risk appetite are those who are eager to be innovative and to choose options offering potentially higher rewards despite greater risk.

How Do Chinese Family Businesses Deal with Risk?

When first arriving in the host countries, such as Indonesia, Thailand, Malaysia, and the Philippines, most Chinese immigrants were in poor condition. They often had to deal with a hostile reception from the host countries. The only thing on their mind at that time was how to survive. This made them willing to take any jobs that were available. Many of them started their own business. For many years, they lived a humble life.

Take Dhanin Chearavanont, the current CEO of Charoen Pokphand, as an example. He came from a humble family. At the time he was born, his father, Chia Ek Chor, had been living in Bangkok, Thailand, for about ten years. When he arrived in Thailand, he brought with him seeds to be planted, to meet the strong demand from Chinese immigrants who have lived there.

Because of the unstable political situation, China in the 1920s was not a favorable place to do business. So it was not surprising that many people left the country and tried to find a new place to live. Dhanin's father and uncle, Chia Ek Chor and Chia Seow Hui, are no exception. Nevertheless, things did not become easier for the two brothers since the situation in Thailand was not much better. Finally, thanks to their perseverance and hard work, as well as their strong relationship with fellow ethnic Chinese, they were able to survive and thrive. Chia Ek Chor focused on running the business in Thailand, while at the same time, his brother marketed the products abroad. They sold seeds and agricultural products. Later we all know that CP becomes one of the largest agricultural companies in the world.

Lee Shin Cheng, the founder of IOI Corporation, also came from a poor family. Lee is the son of a Chinese food shop owner. He spent his childhood in Kuala Lumpur. For some time, he had to stop going to school to help his family, although he could then continue his studies. He was once rejected by one plantation company because of his poor English. However, he did not give up. He sent his application to another company and was finally accepted.

Andrew Tan of the Alliance Global Group, Philippines, was born to poor Chinese immigrant parents, Tan Ha and Soonti Lim. His father worked in a transistor-radio factory, and his mother was a housewife. He spent his childhood in Sta. Cruz, Manila. His father had little formal education and told Andrew not to follow in his footsteps. Andrew's father vowed to put him in school no matter how financially difficult it might be. To secure a better future for him and his family, he studied accounting at the University of the East and graduated magna cum laude. He used to walk from Sta. Cruz in Manila to the University of the East campus because he had no money. When he was in college, many of his classmates were better off than he. They had family businesses of their own. Some owned grocery shops, and others hardware stores. He was envious of their fortune, so he dreamed of becoming a businessman.

Because survival was the main goal, these Chinese immigrants were ready to take and accept any risk. However, this didn't mean that they were not aware of the risk itself. In other words, they became more tolerant regarding the risk involved. They felt that they had nothing to lose. Their willingness to take and accept risk, combined with hard work, perseverance, and camaraderie among Chinese immigrants, made their businesses thrive. Later, as we all know, their businesses played an important role in their economies.

Robert Kuok stresses the importance of courage when someone decides to have his or her own company. Without courage, the business will not grow, and might even die in a short time. This means that someone must not be afraid of risk. Risk exists in every business and always comes with opportunity. The ability to capitalize on opportunity will result in a great reward. The problem is that opportunity often comes only once, not twice.

Later, these Chinese family businesses decided to diversify their business to spread risk. Many of them built a conglomerate, a combination of two or more corporations engaged in entirely different businesses that fall under one corporate structure (a corporate group), usually involving a parent company and several (or many) subsidiaries.

Establishing various businesses is seen as a way to reduce risk. Robert Kuok is one of the people who believes such a thing. He has various businesses specializing in fields such as tourism, media, plantation, transportation, mining, financial services, and trading. When asked why he decided to get into many businesses instead of focusing on only one, Kuok answered that all his businesses are related to each other.

Kuok is not alone in this. Other Chinese family business leaders, such as Sudono Salim, Mochtar Riady, Eka Tjipta (Indonesia); Yeoh Tiong Lay, Lee Shin Cheng (Malaysia); Dhanin Chearavanont, Chin Sophonpanic (Thailand); and John Gokongwei (Philippines), do the same thing.

Their willingness to take risk continued even after their businesses thrived. Take Sudono Salim, for example. The group does not only focus on the domestic market; they entered the overseas market as well. This decision was based on the group's willingness to take risk, combined with sharp business intuition. In 1991, Salim made a US$15.8 million investment in Russia. The First Pacific Company has played an important role regarding Salim's overseas investment. Thanks to Anthony Salim and Manuel Pangilinan, First Pacific Company's Managing Directors until 1999, Salim was interested to buy Hagemeyer in the Netherlands stock exchange. After Hagemeyer was bought by First Pacific Company, Hagemeyer's share price rose sharply, from 26 guilder to 67 guilder. (Guilder was the Dutch currency until it was replaced by the euro on January 1, 2002.)

In 1974, Sudono Salim predicted that technology would drive the business forward. Peter Gontha, an entrepreneur and one of Indonesia's senior music promoters, said, "Salim has a great intuition. Although he was old, Bank Central Asia could thrive thanks to the advanced technology."

Another example is Robert Kuok when he decided to establish Shangri-La Hotel in Hangzhou in the 1980s. At that time, the tourism infrastructure in China was underdeveloped. In such a situation, foreign visitors would be reluctant to come. But Kuok saw things differently. He believed that in the future the tourism sector in China would flourish because the country had an abundant cultural heritage. And he was right. Today there are 34 Shangri-La Hotels. In the world, there are 72 Shangri-La Hotels. There are 45 that are still being built, 28 in China. Kuok stresses the importance of qualified human resources involved in the service sector. So, these people should be given priority. Training and development, as well as good compensation, should be provided.

Dhanin Chearavanont, the CEO of CP who assumed the leadership post from his father in the 1960s, has succeeded in transforming the company into a large corporation through his philosophy of "farm to fork." *Charoen Pokphand* means "prosperity for consumers." Dhanini is known as a visionary and brilliant businessperson. He is very good in reading consumer trends, identifying potential markets and business opportunities, and capitalizing them into profitable businesses. It was CP that set up business in the agricultural sector in 1979, the first multinational company to do so. At that time, economic reform in China, introduced by Deng Xiaoping, had just been started. The company also introduced new farming concepts that revolutionized the farming industry, concepts that are useful for everyone. Dhanin, like other successful businesspersons around the world, is a real entrepreneur, marked with the courage to take a calculated risk. The company has also expanded to other sectors, such as telecommunication and retail.

Risk Attitude among Younger Generations in Chinese Family Businesses

The older generations in Chinese family firms are more tolerant regarding risk. They feel that without any courage to take risk, they will not be able to survive. With such courage, they strove to build their businesses from scratch. Many of them succeeded. Prior to the Asian economic crisis in 1997, many companies under the Salim Group, such as BCA, Indomobil, Salim Plantation, and Indosiar, became prominent players in their respective industries.

However, the younger generations are faced with very different situations. At the time the younger generation takes over control, companies usually have good performance. Business is growing, market share is big, and financial conditions and position are sound. Younger generations want to maintain such good performance. Therefore, they will be more careful regarding business decisions, particularly when expanding their business. They do not want to put the company's performance at risk.

Younger generations also have better educations compared to the older generation. Many of them attended some of the best schools in the world, particularly in western countries. They also have outside working experience prior to joining the family business. As the result, they tend to be more familiar with modern risk-management concepts, which emphasize a more careful approach regarding risk. They then adopt these new concepts, together with other modern management practices.

At the time the younger generation is handed the power, the surrounding environment is changing rapidly. Competition is more intense, demands from stakeholders are increasing, and political situations are changing. In such situations, any mistake in decision making will be more costly. In the worst case, it could also damage the company and family reputation, something that ethnic Chinese want to avoid at all costs.

Good performance, better education, and a changing environment have made the younger generations less tolerant of risk. Their risk appetite is also lower. However, this does not mean they avoid risk completely. It is just that they are more calculating in taking risks. They realize that without any courage to take risk, the business is not going to thrive.

Instead of entering many kinds of businesses, Chinese family businesses led by younger generations tend to be more focused. They tend to be less aggressive. Salim Group is one example. After political reform following Suharto's resignation in 1998, Salim Group's business strategy changed drastically. Once a large conglomerate, today Salim Group has become a more focused business. In the past, the group was involved in many industries, such as telecommunications, consumer goods, cement, and banking. Salim Group has abandoned its financial and media businesses, and has sold its ownership in Indosiar, a TV station in Indonesia. However, its consumer goods (such as Bogasari and Indofood) and cement businesses are still maintained since they have been the core strength of the group.

Apparently, Salim Group is now more comfortable being involved in a business with lower exposure; its business exposure is no longer focused on the group but is focused more on its individual businesses. In other words, it adopts low-profile businesses. Its executives also avoid the overexposure of their products in the market as it could potentially create a negative image.

Chapter 10

Issues on Sustainability in Family Businesses

F amily business success is often acknowledged by how long the company or group is owned by the family. How many generations the business is able to be sustained would be the primary goal of the company. Family performance is not only measured by the amount of return, or expansion of the business, but also by the longevity of the business.

Phases of Growth in a Family Business

Every family business undergoes the following four phases of growth: 1. *developing phase;* 2. *managing phase;* 3. *transforming phase;* and 4. *sustaining phase.* As the business grows bigger, the challenge is how to transform and sustain it.

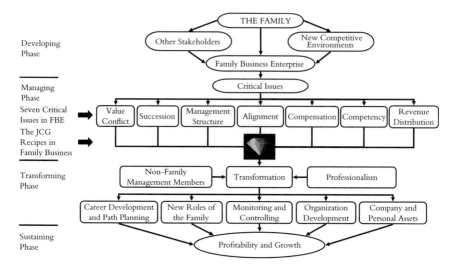

Figure 10.1   Model for managing growth in a family business

The Jakarta Consulting Group has developed a model for managing growth in a family business through each phase, as shown in Figure 10.1.

In the developing phase, the family members are the main driving force for the business. The development of the business is also influenced by stakeholders such as customers, employees, and the surrounding community, as well as the competitive environment.

As a family business enters the managing phase, there are seven critical issues that need to be addressed: value conflict, succession, management structure, alignment, compensation, competency, and revenue distribution.

In the transforming phase, non-family management members are brought into the business. Non-family management members can bring fresh ideas, including how to prepare career development and career paths for family members. In this phase, the company should address new roles for the family members—monitoring and controlling, organizational development, and personal assets. Monitoring and controlling have to be done to ensure that family expectations are met. The organizational development is a company-wide effort to increase the organization's effectiveness and viability. In a family business there is often no clear separation between business and personal assets. Nevertheless, separating personal assets from business assets is necessary to avoid negative consequences. Success in undergoing this process requires support from family members, understanding from professionals regarding family members' perspectives and point of view, behavior adjustment, and harmonious cooperation.

If a family business is able to undergo these three phases, profitability and growth can be achieved in the sustaining phase. In this phase, all systems, procedures, and organizational policies have been well-established and well-implemented. The company no longer depends on a personal or family figure. Instead, it relies on the system, which is continuously being improved.

Challenges in Maintaining Sustainability

Many family businesses are unable to reach the sustaining phase. They have to be closed down due to failing during the transforming phase. It means they are unable to create the right organizational structure, system, and procedure, as well as recruiting competent professionals and developing human resource policy. They have also failed to address the seven critical issues in a family business.

One of the reasons why many family businesses fail in the transforming phase is their resistance to change. The family business owner usually already feels comfortable with the current situation, so there is no need to make any change. Family relations may also impede change because it is considered a threat to the family harmony.

Resistance to change might also be caused by the fear of losing acquired competencies, as well as the possible loss of established allocation and resources. Structural, cultural, and policy changes can be followed by changes in jobs and positions, which can be perceived as estranging a family relationship that has been established.

Change is inevitable if a family business wants to move forward. However, change needs support from family members and employees. Kenny Yap from Qian Hu said that the key factor of their company's success is the acceptance of his leadership by the rest of the family members and their "willingness and eagerness to try new concepts and methods in the business" (*Asian Entrepreneur*, March/April 1999, p. 119). Yap also said in the interview that "an entrepreneur must be ready to change the culture of his industry by introducing new ways of doing things."

Families that do not always protect themselves from criticism, exposure to shortcomings, or a perceived threat to the ego—as well as have strong motivation to solve any problem—will have a bigger chance to succeed compared with those that have problems with denial, defensiveness, and disagreement. Some of them do not have the resources, patience, and courage to make a change. Successful family businesses are those that create a new future for the family as well as the business, foster openness and optimism, and have energy and resources to make necessary changes.

Another reason is the tendency to keep too many secrets. There is a notion, not only from the employees but from the family members as well, that many overseas Chinese family businesses (OCFBs) tend to keep too many secrets regarding information about the management. This might be caused by several factors. First, there is the fear that there will be competitors who will take advantage of the information regarding the family business's internal conditions. Second, the company is afraid that employees will leave after they find out about the company's weaknesses. Third, the leaders feel guilty because the company has made a big profit or revenue while at the same time not providing good compensation for the employees.

Whatever the reason, keeping too many secrets could undermine trust, weaken company morale, and produce substandard performance. In the end, many of the company's best talents leave. Too many secrets can also spark conflict among family members. Remember that employees need sufficient information so that they can work well. Therefore, the company should provide its employees with accurate, complete, timely, and actual information. We can say that excessive secrecy might become the root of the family firm's inability to sustain.

Such inability and failure result in:

1. Unfair workload distribution, compensation, and benefits
2. Resistance to non-family professionals and nepotism
3. Absence of leadership and succession plan
4. Generation gap and conflict of interest
5. Inability of the senior generation to let go

6. Lack of commitment and tangible recognition
7. Elements of distrust and dysfunctional relationships
8. Consumerism and generational decline

We will discuss each of these points next, including its relevance to overseas Chinese family businesses.

Unfair Workload Distribution, Compensation, and Benefits

Workload means the amount of work assigned to, or expected from, a worker in a specified time period. In many family businesses, unfair workload is often the result of the lack of a clear job description, organizational structure, roles and procedures, and reporting relationships, as well as the concentration of decision-making in the hands of family members. We can find such characteristics in many Chinese family firms. Unfair compensation and benefits is the result of unfair performance evaluation. Chinese family businesses should be aware of this because there are still many of them that consider seniority and personal relationships in evaluating performance, rather than the quality of work.

In many Chinese family businesses, criteria for compensation are mainly based on the ownership and family relationships rather than individual performance. The problem is that many family members still receive their compensation although they are not involved in the business. Such situations can create a rift and feelings of injustice among family members and non-family professionals as well.

Compensation problems seldom emerge when the business is still run by the founder, while at the same time the younger generation is starting to enter the business. Any dissatisfaction can be quickly resolved by the founder. However, since the second generations usually consist of brothers and sisters—who start to hold various managerial positions—complaints about compensation start to emerge. For example, one family member considers compensation received by his siblings as unfair considering the workload. The company must not neglect any compensation issue since it could create dissatisfaction among family members.

Seniority, reliability, and trustworthiness play a more important role in managing human resources in many Chinese family businesses.

However, as the family business grows and professionals from outside the family start to join, performance should become the primary consideration. This also should be applied to the family members. Remember that professionals outside of the family—who have many of the competencies needed by the family business and part of generation Y—expect a clear career path, good compensation, fair performance evaluation, and a wide opportunity for career and personal development. If such things cannot be found in a family business, they certainly feel disappointed and dissatisfied. This increases the turnover rate, and many of the company's best talents leave.

Resistance to Non-Family Professionals and Nepotism

As a result of growth and development, outside professionals must be recruited to strengthen the family firm. Unfortunately, the inclusion of non-family professionals often creates discomfort for some family members. They are in fear of loss of power and control. This makes them reluctant to delegate some of their authority in managing the business to more competent people outside the family. The family members often do not give non-family professionals enough authority to make strategic planning decisions. However, they should overcome this feeling of discomfort. Strengthening the family bond is important, but can be done for the wrong reasons, such as nepotism.

Nepotism is favoritism granted to families and relatives regardless of merit. In nepotism, business logics take a backseat to family concerns. Nepotism often stems from the family founder's decision to include an incompetent family member. Recruiting family members into the company can be justified as long as they have the necessary competencies. Unfortunately, the senior leaders often turn a blind eye to the family members' weaknesses and inability. This will create an unfair human resource management practice. As a result, family businesses become an unattractive workplace for non-family professionals. The situation will get worse if there is unfair compensation. Employees will feel that they are treated unfairly. In turn, this will undermine trust, one of the basic elements in a healthy organization. Low trust undermines employee satisfaction, motivation, and performance. The situation will become ironic if the family members demand a high commitment from all employees. This can be justified if the family business leaders provide fair rewards for the non-family employees due to their achievements and contributions. But such demands will not be acceptable when rewards are not given based on performance and contribution to the company.

Eu Yan Sang is an example of an OCFB that has abandoned nepotism. Since the third generation took over the leadership post, the operations of the company have been handled by professionals, who were able to contribute to the growth and development of the company. The professionals were given more trust and autonomy to manage the business. The fourth generation took a further step by appointing professionals to the senior leadership positions.

Kenny Yap from Qian Hu is apparently aware of the negative consequences of nepotism. Qian Hu often faces difficulty in attracting the best professionals into the family business because they have negative perceptions about career prospects (Fock and Wilkinson, 2007). Hence, Qian Hu has taken steps to gradually separate the management and ownership of the company so that it can be more professionally run.

Regarding the separation between management and ownership, in one Nanyang Business School—*Business Times* roundtable discussion Fock, one of the senior professors at Nanyang Technological University, says that a family business structure is made up of three independent and overlapping subsystems, namely business, ownership, and family. The three subsystems create a lot of tension, for example, for an individual who is at the same time a family member, an owner, and a manager of the family business. When such tensions are not appropriately managed, the family business structure becomes a source of interpersonal conflicts and explosive negative expressions among the different stakeholders of the family business.

Absence of Leadership and Succession Plan

Andrew Tan from Alliance Global Group once said, "Success is not the doing of one man alone; it is the hard work of many. For success to happen you must have the ability to inspire others to work with and for you; you must be able to inspire them to give you their best."

What Andrew said is actually the essence of leadership. Unfortunately, there are still many Chinese family business leaders who do not realize it. Although the business environment has changed rapidly, many Chinese family business leaders tend to maintain their paternalistic style, where the relationship is arranged on a hierarchical basis. Leaders make all key decisions. They do not trust anyone except the closest family members. Janine Tay, the founder of Hour Glass, Singapore, had an experience with her husband's family watch shop, Lee Chay and Co. Watch Shop. Lee Chay was conservatively managed by the first generation, who did not trust non-family members. She finally decided to leave and established Orchard Watch Company and later Hour Glass in 1979.

Paternalistic style can be maintained as long as leaders have outstanding expertise and are the only source of information needed to manage all aspects of business. However, this will never be the case, particularly with the advanced development of ICT.

Paternalistic style has disadvantages also. The company will rely too heavily on the leaders, ignore training and development programs for younger generations, and fail to manage complexity and ambiguity. Used to being dictated to and told what to do and how to do it, employees working in a family business with a paternalistic style of leadership will feel incompetent and powerless. Paternalistic leadership can be successfully implemented only in a stable environment. However, in today's business environment, this is no longer the case.

Another disadvantage of paternalistic style is its tendency to restrict employees' initiative and creativity since family members and employees are too dependent on the senior leaders. Unfortunately, initiative and creativity are needed to survive and win the business competition.

A good leader is someone who can prepare future successors through a good succession plan. However, poor leadership and lack of succession planning are difficult issues in any family firm. Again, succession planning is not simply about transferring power from the older generation to the younger one. It's not about transferring wealth. Succession is related to many aspects of planning, such as ownership succession, managerial succession, strategic planning, and retirement strategy for the senior generation as they enter other phases of their lives. Succession needs time to be implemented and like any plan there's the need to have a contingency plan. All parties involved in the succession need to be ready emotionally and prepare for the worst.

Generation Gap and Conflict of Interest

A generation gap emerges as the result of unresolved multigenerational issues. One of them includes the unwillingness of older generations to share power with the younger ones. The older generations do not acknowledge the maturity and expertise of the younger ones. Another issue is that successors do not have high motivation to improve the company. They do not receive enough support from the owners or seniors and are involved only in insignificant decision making.

Another reason why the generation gap emerges is vision. Soriano (2012) states that first-generation founders might have a certain vision of the children owning the business and working together to continue the business in the future. It might not be acceptable within the family to question the feasibility of this vision. Any conversation about shareholder agreements or the possibility of family members exiting is perceived to be too sensitive. But what if the children do not have the same vision as their parents?

Family plays a very important role in Chinese culture. However, when it comes to business matters, a family often has to do a delicate balancing act between family and business interest. Unfortunately, many family businesses tend to put business interests after family interests. They spend most of their time dealing with family matters due to disagreements and are reluctant to identify future business opportunities. Disagreements can lead to bitter conflict. Such situations often emerge at a time when the family business is experiencing high growth and has succeeded in accumulating wealth. At this point, the conflict of interest within the family will intensify. *Conflict of interest* can be defined as a situation that has the potential to undermine the impartiality of a person because of the possibility of a clash between the person's self-interest and professional or public interest. Family members would tend to take more care of their own property, rather than the property of the business, which could lead to a conflict of interest. For example, say there is a family member who set up her own business that specializes in the same field as the business run by her family. If not addressed properly, this could become a source of conflict. Therefore, family agreement is needed to regulate the rights and obligations of each family member regarding business activities.

Inability of the Senior Generation to Let Go

For senior generations, passing down entrepreneurial spirit to the next generation may not be as difficult as passing down the company's leadership. As a result, many members of senior generations still intervene in the daily business operations although they have announced their resignation. This is because they still have a high sense of belonging and still love their work and business. Many of them are even reluctant to take a day off from work. They think about their business during their vacation. Therefore, it is not surprising that after handing over control to the younger generations, they do not know what they are going to do after succession. However, this intervention could create confusion among employees.

The unwillingness of senior generations to hand over their power to their successors could spark conflict. When the time has come, the senior generation has to think about pursuing activities outside the family business. On the other hand, younger generations must not underestimate their predecessor. They must respect their predecessor's legacy. For Chinese family businesses that still adhere to Confucian teachings, which emphasize submission and devotion to the parents, this should not be a problem. But even for OCFBs that have integrated into the larger culture, the suggestion not to underestimate the predecessor's legacy is still relevant, considering that in order for a transfer of power to be smooth, the involvement of the senior generation is needed.

Lack of Commitment and Tangible Recognition

Senior generations sometimes complain that their children lack the commitment to do their best for the company. They do not work as hard as the senior generation does. However, this does not necessarily mean that the children do not care about the family business. There are reasons why children of the founder might not have to work for long hours like their parents used to do. Usually, children start their full involvement at a time when the business is growing and the number of employees is increasing. Tasks that used to be done by the parents themselves now can be delegated to more qualified persons. This is actually a positive development, as long as the company stands on the "right man in the right place" principle.

Another reason is that there are differences between children and parents regarding entrepreneurial spirit and skills. Children have better managerial skills, while their parents have better entrepreneurial skills. An entrepreneur is more willing to take risk; does not like behavioral, structure, and system rigidity; and is better at capitalizing on opportunities. On the other hand, a manager tends to be more prudent. Nevertheless, an entrepreneur must possess good managerial skills so that he can accomplish his vision. Likewise, a manager must always enhance his entrepreneurial skills to manage change and innovation. The combination of these two skills will add greater value to the company.

Chou Cheng Ngok from Popular Holdings sees that he has to lead in cultivating a sense of both entrepreneurship and professional standards in his company (Fock and Wilkinson, 2007). His goal has always been to create a "corporate entrepreneurial culture" at Popular, and for his staff to act in an entrepreneurial manner. While he has encouraged the professionalization of his company's management team, he feels that his non-family professional managers can be further developed to be entrepreneurs, too.

Elements of Distrust and Dysfunctional Relationships

Although everything seems fine, that does not mean that distrust does not exist. Neglecting this will create an unfavorable condition. Distrust could spark conflict. Conflict will create confusion and disturb the company operation. Therefore, it needs to be checked whether open communication and transparency have been practiced and whether family members and employees are feeling satisfied and appreciated.

To find out the answer to these questions a family business needs to gather opinions from the employees and family members. By doing this, problems can be identified, as well as their root cause. The company must learn what is emerging not only on the surface, but below it as well. In this case, meeting with each individual becomes important.

The company must also create transparency. *Transparency* is a set of information, privacy, and business policies to improve corporate decision making and make operations visible to employees, stakeholders, shareholders, and the general public. Charoen Pokphand (CP) has made an effort to achieve a high degree of financial transparency, including publicly listing a number of its key businesses.

Consumerism and Generational Decline

Consumerism could have two meanings. First, it refers to the movement seeking to protect and inform consumers by requiring such practices as honest packaging and advertising, product guarantees, and improved safety standards. Second, it refers to a social and economic order that encourages the purchase of goods and services in greater amounts. The discussion about consumerism in this chapter refers to this second meaning.

Consumerism is an international phenomenon. Many people purchase goods and consume materials in excess of their basic needs. More specifically, *consumerism* is used to describe the tendency of people to identify strongly with products or services they consume, especially those with commercial brand names and perceived status symbols, such as (but not limited to) luxury cars, designer clothing, expensive jewelry, and expensive ICT gadgets. Consumerism can take extreme forms such that consumers sacrifice significant time and income to purchase expensive but unimportant goods and services.

Consumerism is a common phenomenon, and overseas Chinese society is no exception, particularly the younger generations. Despite its positive effects on the economy, such as an increase in production, higher economic growth, and better living style, consumerism also has negative effects, particularly on individuals, such as productivity decline, short-term orientation, and a lack of saving for future needs. This is in contrast with the characteristics of successful OCFB founders. These founders have taught their children about hard work, long-term orientation, and frugality. They have done this for the sake of their children. If consumerism is embraced by the children of OCFB founders, it could potentially threaten the future performance of the business as well as the harmony in the family.

Consumerism in overseas Chinese society might have a lot to do with what Amy Chua (2011) calls "generational decline." In her book, *Battle Hymn of the Tiger Mother*, Chua explains the common pattern of Chinese immigrants who have come to the United States as graduate students or skilled workers over the last 50 years. The first immigrants were the hardest workers; they worked very hard to become successful engineers, scientists, doctors, academicians, and businesspeople. As parents, they were very strict. The next generation is the first that was born in the United States. This generation is typically characterized by high achievers. They attend the best universities, tend to be professionals, and surpass their parents in income, but this is because they started off with more money and because their parents invested so much in them. Then comes the most worrisome generation—the third generation. Because of the hard work of their parents and grandparents, this generation will be born into the great comfort of the upper-middle class. They will have wealthy friends, expect expensive clothes, and be much more likely to disobey their parents and ignore career advice.

Chua is not a family business leader. Her observation is limited to Chinese immigrants in the United States. Nevertheless, such phenomena might also occur in other places, particularly in a region where the number of overseas Chinese is large and the economy is growing, such as the Southeast Asia region. Moreover, the presence of overseas Chinese in this region has a long history. Therefore, OCFBs should be aware of the generational decline, as well as consumerism.

Chapter 11

Suggestions for Developing Chinese Family Businesses

V alues such as strong family relationships, trustworthiness, hard work, and frugality have been the foundation of success for many Chinese family businesses. However, that will not be enough. Like any other business, Chinese family businesses need to implement the right management techniques and principles, particularly as the business grows and develops. Therefore, modernization is inevitable. Succession plans should be developed. Estate planning should be developed. Conflict management and resolution must be implemented. However, modernization, succession plans, conflict management, and conflict resolution will not succeed without good corporate governance, the right business paradigm, strategy, structure, and system, as well as competent family members, qualified professional managers, fair

remuneration, equal treatment, the right leadership, strong commitment, and strategy renewal. Ethical behavior and corporate social
responsibility should also be promoted.

Implementing Corporate Governance

Successful overseas Chinese family businesses (OCFBs) implement good
corporate governance. Corporate governance directs the company's
attention toward the improvement of performance through supervision
and monitoring. It also ensures the accountability of management to the
company's stakeholders. Corporate governance can also motivate
management to enhance its effectiveness and control the behavior of
managers so that they always put the stakeholders' interest ahead of their
own. Corporate governance includes fairness, transparency, accountability, and responsibility. Company leaders have to be fair when dis-
tributing money to the shareholders. There should be openness and
transparency regarding the company's policies and who should be
accountable for the policies. Executives should be given greater
authority to develop the business.

Family firms can start their corporate governance by defining the
family and business goals, and then combining the goals with accountability, which is the focus of corporate governance. Corporate governance
structure in a family business usually consists of the family and its institutions, such as family assembly, family council, shareholders' committee,
board of directors, and executive committee. The family, as the owner of
the business, should be responsible for handling corporate governance
issues.

There are still not many OCFBs implementing corporate governance. However, it is needed as the company grows and more family
members and non-family professionals join the business.

One's tasks and responsibilities in a family business are usually based
on the appointment by family members or advice regarding the company's basic structure.

Usually, there are three basic structures needed in a family business,
namely Family Council, Audit Committee, and Advisory Council, as

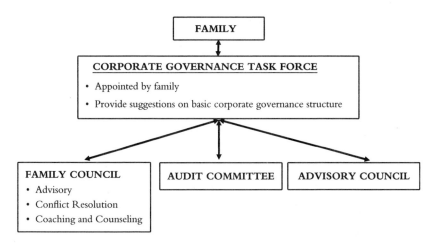

Figure 11.1   Family business governance structure

shown in Figure 11.1. A family council is usually run by a management consultant acting as the advisor, conflict mediator, and training and counseling provider. Family council is needed to change the organizational structure of the family business, which usually hasn't met the common standard, and also to resolve any conflict. An audit committee is needed to audit the family business. The audit comittee examines weaknesess in the family business. An advisory council will provide the family business with legal assistance. It also provides assistance related to agreements, share distribution, and succession.

To achieve a successful corporate government, a family business must address six issues. First, the selection of managers: The company should select the right managers, ones who must be able to lead and serve as role models for their subordinates. Second, integrity of management: Managing a family business requires a common understanding about the vision and mission and what the family and employees should do to achieve them. High commitment from family members is important to unite the perspectives and goals. Third, responsibility of management: The family members and non-family managers should be accountable for every action they take. Therefore, they must think carefully before making any decision regarding company policy. Fourth, accountability of the audit committee: Without accountability, the audit result will not be valid, since it is not in accordance with the applied standard. Fifth, transparency on accounting reports: This emphasizes the importance of transparent financial reporting in managing a company. Transparency and honesty is the basic foundation for success. Without transparency and honesty, a company cannot earn trust. And sixth, adherence to commitment and agreements made: Any commitment or agreement should be fulfilled so that trust and integrity can be earned.

One OCFB that states its belief in corporate governance is Charoen Pokphand (CP). Dhanin Chearavanont, the current CEO, as quoted by Vorabandhit (2004), said, "The smaller the business, the more it belongs to the family. The larger the business, the more it belongs to society. Therefore, large business should be very transparent. For example, if accounting is not transparent, no one will dare give a loan to that business."

Creating a New Business Paradigm, Strategy, Structure, and System

Along with growth and development, a Chinese family business must change the paradigm and way of thinking. It is wrong to think that a family business can naturally grow and develop without having to implement modern management techniques and principles. After changing toward the right paradigm, the family business needs to improve its strategy, as well as its structure and system, to accomplish its vision and mission. The right structure and system will clarify the responsibility, authority, rights, and obligations of each family member and employee. If not designed properly, it would be difficult for the company to handle many activities, such as recruiting competent employees, serving its customers, managing inventories, maintaining the company's assets, and handling customer complaints. As a result, the image of the family business could be tarnished since it is considered unable to serve its customers well, employee' morale will weaken, and customers will prefer to buy the competitor's product.

According to Daft (2004), organizational structure must provide a framework of responsibilities, reporting relationships, and groups, and it must provide mechanisms for linking and coordinating organizational elements into a coherent whole. He also says that managers can choose whether to orient toward a traditional organization designed for efficiency, which emphasizes vertical linkages such as hierarchy, rules and plans, and formal information systems, or toward a contemporary learning organization, which emphasizes horizontal communication and coordination.

Whichever is chosen, there is no one-size-fits-all organizational structure. Instead, a structure must be aligned with a strategy. In other words, structure must follow strategy. Such alignment enables an organization to make adjustments, to set clearer and more understandable goals and objectives, promote employee participation in decision making, and improve communication.

Unfortunately, an organizational structure has often already existed even before the strategy is set. This could create lack of alignment in the company. Lack of alignment could potentially delay decision making, undermine the decision quality, and cause failure to adjust to environmental change. It also could create doubt among employees regarding company direction, and waste the company's resources.

Michael Widjaja from Sinarmas Land said that in order to thrive, strong organization is needed so that expertise and product excellence can be developed. Systems and processes should be optimized so that the company will be more effective and efficient. Sinarmas Land created a new organization that merges two publicly listed companies, namely PT Bumi Serpong Damai Tbk and PT Duta Pertiwi Tbk. Sinarmas Land improves the work process, restructures operating systems, and harmonizes the business process. Michael Widjaja created a new organizational structure for Sinarmas Land based on the similarity in business units and core competence so that cooperation among departments or functions can be enhanced. The value chain process will start from Strategic Land Bank (SLB). Its main duty is to propose development concepts to the executive committee and to create a master plan. In creating a master plan, SLB receives input from Residential, Commercial, Asset Management, and Corporate Strategy and Services. SLB is responsible for external relations, legal, permits, and certificates, as well as estate management.

To support the transformation, a new division called Project Management Office (PMO) is set up to help the organization maximize its performance. Corporate Strategy and Services is responsible for marketing communications, business development, procurement and general services reengineering, information technology, and so forth.

Sinarmas Land will become an integrated company that grows with various products and segments. Sinarmas Land has a vision: to become the most trusted real estate developer in Indonesia. Sinarmas Land gives each of its business units a way to focus on being the best. Strategic Land Bank will focus its attention on creating long-term value-added products and services. Residential, Commercial, and Asset management business units will focus their attention on achieving current financial results. Project Support Services will ensure the quality of the products. Other corporate functions such as finance and human resources will also add value to Sinarmas Land as a whole.

Enhancing Education and Competence for Family Members

One factor impeding the success of a family business is the lack of professionals among family members. The company must anticipate this by providing the best education for the next generations so that they will have better skills and knowledge. Fortunately, senior generations in many Chinese family businesses are aware of this. They send their children to the world's best universities and higher education institutions. This is in stark contrast with the first generation, many of whom never went to a university. There are so many examples we can mention here: Joshua Yeoh, the son of Francis Yeoh from YTL, graduated from Cambridge University with a master's degree in civil engineering. His sister, Ruth Yeoh, graduated from the University of Nottingham, which consistently ranks among the top ten schools in the UK in the most highly regarded world and national rankings. Currently, she is the executive director of YTL Singapore Pte. Ltd.

Another example is Chartsiri Sophonpanich, the first son of Chatri Sophonpanich and grandson of Chin Sophonpanich, the founder of Bangkok Bank. Chartsiri was educated in the United States at the Massachusetts Institute of Technology, where he obtained an MS in chemical engineering and an MS in management from the MIT Sloan

School of Management. After working at Citibank in New York, he returned to Thailand to join Bangkok Bank on February 1, 1986. He gained extensive experience at both operational and managerial levels in various departments at Bangkok Bank, including Foreign Exchange Trading, Marketing, Treasury, Investment Banking Group, and International Banking Group, before being appointed president on December 1, 1994.

Lance Gokongwei, the son of John Gokongwei, the founder of JG Summit Holdings, holds a bachelor of science in finance and Applied science from the University of Pennsylvania, Wharton School. He attended the Management and Technology Program at the University of Pennsylvania.

Rayvin Tan, the son of Vincent Tan from Berjaya, Malaysia, graduated with a bachelor of science (First Class Honors) degree in accounting and finance from the London School of Economics (LSE), United Kingdom, in 2000. LSE is one of the most prestigious schools in the world.

Suphachai Chearavanont, the son of Dhanin Chearavanont from CP, holds a bachelor of science in business administration, majoring in financial management, from Boston University.

Recruiting Non-Family Executive Professional Managers

Every family business must have managers or professionals from outside the family to avoid bias and subjectivity. In addition, professional managers could promote professionalism.

Non-family professionals provide new information, expertise, and experience. They support accountability in management. They can help evaluate ideas and strategies. They can give clear, honest, and objective views. They can create image and professional relationships within the external environment.

In many family businesses, leaders and employees still work long hours although the productivity does not improve significantly. Non-family professionals could help family members change work-hard principles into work-smart principles, where leaders and employees work normal hours while at the same time improving productivity significantly.

Many Chinese family businesses even recruit outside directors or executives. Competent outside directors are valuable resources for a family business. They can help the family business to improve its strategy and ensure the continuity of business operations.

Many transitions would not be successful without the help of outside directors. Outside directors can help family members and employees in eliminating the fear of a rough transition by inspiring commitment and providing momentum for the older generation to step down and for the younger one to start taking over the control.

When the second, third, or even the fourth generations own and manage the business together, outside directors can help each family member in finding continuous consensus. When some family members work in the company and some don't, an outside director could give objective views regarding dividends, compensation, and performance.

Recruiting outside directors to work in the family business brings the following advantages:

1. Outside directors provide fresh and creative perspective. Their experience and knowledge will spur family members' creativity.
2. Outside directors can give objective feedback and opinions.
3. Outside directors can help family members in solving problems regarding roles. Family business owners or leaders often play multiple roles. Sometimes they cannot differentiate whether their opinion or action represents the perspective of the individual, family, manager, or owner.
4. Outside directors promote discipline and accountability, resulting in higher standards and improved performance.
5. Outside directors usually inspire family business owners or leaders with greater self-confidence regarding their thoughts and abilities.
6. Outside directors help family members comprehend the importance of succession planning. The fear that the company will be sold will disappear. Financial institutions, investors, and suppliers will feel more secure.
7. The presence of outside directors shows that family business owners or leaders are open to new ideas.

Nowadays, more and more Chinese family businesses have appointed non-family members as directors or CEOs. YTL is one of them. In November 2011, Kemmy Tan Peck Mun was appointed as CEO of YTL Land and Development Berhad. Kemmy leads the group's property portfolio in the region while strategizing new avenues for the group's future growth and development. Prior to joining the YTL Group, Kemmy was general manager of Sentosa Cove, Singapore's pioneer and only integrated marina residential development, responsible for the marketing, development, and estate management of the 117-hectare development. She previously held senior marketing and business positions in listed and private entities, including CapitaLand Ltd., Tuan Sing Holdings, and Far East Organization, with wide-ranging experience across the residential, commercial, retail, and industrial property sectors. Kemmy graduated from National University of Singapore in 1991, where she obtained a bachelor of science (with honors) in estate management, and also holds a graduate diploma in marketing. She is a council member of the Real Estate Developers' Association of Singapore (REDAS) Management Committee and is the chairwoman of its seminar committee.

If non-family professionals are recruited to the company, particularly for the top-level position, they always want to know everything about the business and the company. Therefore, transparency becomes important. These non-family professionals should also be motivated through good incentives, good career development planning, clear and fair performance measures, and a favorable climate.

On the other hand, it is also important for non-family professionals to understand the family point of view so that change can be easier and smoother. Non-family professionals need to show a certain degree of tolerance. This means that they should not insist on their ideas being implemented immediately.

Analyzing Corporate Life Cycle

By analyzing corporate life cycle, a family business can identify its strengths and weaknesses. It can also help the business in anticipating unexpected events, as well as managing continuity in the future.

Generally, a corporate life cycle begins with the creation stage and continues with the growth, maturity, and declining stages. At the creation stage, a company introduces its products and services for the first time. There are still no organizational structures, systems, and procedures. The number of employees is relatively small. The company focuses on survival.

In the growth stage, income increases, as well as the number of employees. More products and services are introduced. At this stage, the company must create organizational structure, system, and procedure. For a family business, this is the stage where younger generations and extended family start to join and play an active role, as well as non-family professionals. The key success factor in this stage is to have a coordinated and harmonized team in the top management structure. Professionals need to be competent in administration, system development, control, and risk management; in other words, they need to complement the family entrepeneurial spirit.

In the maturity stage, the growth rate is relatively stable. The structure, system, and procedure are steady. The company's priority is to maintain market share. This stage can last for a long time, even without time limits. However, the loss of a leading product, the rise of substitute products, big debt, and resistance to change can lead the business toward the declining stage or even its demise if the decline fails to stop. To prevent such things from happening, the declining trends should be reversed. Strategy, structure, system, and procedure should be reviewed.

In the maturity stage, a family business must be aware of the decline in innovation and lack of new ideas, as well as excessive formalities and rituals. The company focuses itself on internal problems and loses touch with its customers. It is also very proud of its past success, without realizing that the environment has changed.

Promoting Fair Remuneration and Equal Treatment among Members

Remuneration should be tied to performance, which should be applied to both family members and non-family employees. Equal treatment should be applied regardless of seniority, relationships with the family, and so on. Fair remuneration and equal treatment will minimize potential conflict in the family business.

Henry Sy, Jr. from SM Prime Holdings, Inc. once said, "We believe in treating people fair and square, so that our efforts would be rewarded with our customers' loyalty." He also argues that being good is not limited to their interaction with clients. It's also the central pillar on which the corporate culture is founded. "We have to internalize how to be good from within. After all, you can only be creative and service-oriented when you feel good about your company," he says.

In Panda Express, Andrew Cherng pays his starting employees at least 50 cents more than the minimum wage and promotes people within the company. Almost three quarters of Panda Express managers were originally hired for a lower position. Such opportunity allows Cherng to select from the cream of the crop and reduce training costs by retaining valued and experienced workers. This policy is a contradiction to the popular belief that the Chinese entrepreneur is stingy and is a slave-driver.

Chreng requires his managers to be able to encourage followers under their supervision so that they will have a strong commitment to the company. He also wants his top managers to adjust their behaviors so that they are in line with the company's culture. To ensure this, he is not reluctant to give feedback by talking directly to them. For Cherng, top managers must not only focus on their work, but also other activities outside the office. These top managers must never stop learning. Employees who do not have good attitudes should be dismissed, although they may have strong skills and knowledge.

There is a unique story from Unilab, Philippines. Its huge labor force has never had a labor union similar to other huge industrial firms in the Philippines or Southeast Asia. Unilab is fair and generous to its workers and even to its retirees.

Influencing with the Right Leadership

A family business needs leadership that can help ensure its stability, continuity, and successful change. Change is not easy for a family business. To overcome this difficulty, a family business could build consensus regarding the importance of developing leadership; determine rights, obligations, and leadership processes; manage governance for effective decision making and fair dispute resolution; and implement a strategic plan.

As the family business grows and develops, it is impossible to depend only on one figure. Collective leadership will help family members to get more involved. Many Chinese family businesses have collective leadership. It is not unusual to see the founder's children hold the top leadership positions in the family business, such as in Lippo (Indonesia), YTL (Malaysia), and SM Investments Corporation (Philippines). Collectiveness in the family should be maintained.

A successful family business usually appreciates any approach. It also accommodates informal groups through greater understanding and involvement. Informal groups emerge naturally due to the response and common interests of the members of an organization who can easily identify with the goals or independent activities of the group.

Disputes and conflicts often happen in a family business. Therefore, leaders of family businesses should develop a mechanism for dispute resolution to avoid bigger and more bitter conflicts. Conflict threatens family harmony and the company's existence. Many family businesses collapse because of bitter conflicts.

Leaders of family businesses should know the strengths and weaknesses of themselves, family members, and the other people working in the company so that they can put everyone in the right position and the right job. A fair recruitment, selection, and compensation policy is a must to avoid jealousy among family members.

Reformulating Strategy and Renewing Business

Only by reformulating strategy and renewing the business can the family business maintain its competitiveness. Leaders must support every change initiative toward greater progress and prosperity. Charoen Pokphand is a good example. CP has learned its lessons from the economic crisis that hit Southeast Asian countries in 1997, since the agribusiness company was badly affected by the falling of Southeast Asian currencies. CP realized that it had been involved in too many businesses. Therefore, it decided to restructure them to improve its performance. CP abandoned some of its businesses such as Lotus Supercenter (which was sold to Tesco in Britain), Ek Chor Motorcycle subsidiary in Shanghai, China, and some of TelecomAsia (TA)'s subsidiaries. It also strived to improve its financial position and condition, and aimed to reduce its debt to a manageable level. CP also decided to concentrate its resources towards agribusiness. It has made efforts to enhance efficiency by merging 11 of its agribusiness subsidiaries.

Today, CP has become a world-class company. It is one of the world's largest producers in animal feeds, shrimp-related products, and poultry. For his achievements in making CP an admired company, Dhanin Chearavanont, the company's CEO, was awarded *Forbes Asia's* 2011 "Businessman of the Year."

Ciputra has decided to focus on the property sector and to develop his business to big cities outside the Java island, Indonesia. This means he no longer diversifies his business to unrelated sectors. He wants to build commercial property projects in many cities and countries, including Asia and the Middle East. He actively gives direction regarding vision, mission, and strategies in his businesses. Currently, Ciputra serves as president commissioner in three groups, namely Ciputra Group, Metropolitan Group, and Jaya Group.

Promoting Ethical Behavior

When making business decisions, ethical behavior must not be ignored. Basically, ethics is moral standards about right and wrong, good and bad.

For a company, promoting ethical behavior means avoiding breaking the law, avoiding actions and activities causing a lawsuit from any stakeholder, and avoiding actions and activities that could tarnish the company's image. Promoting ethical behavior is extremely important for Chinese family businesses that want to enhance their glory and reputation.

Ignoring ethical behavior will bring negative consequences. Employees' morale will deteriorate since they have to carry the psychological burden of working for a company that has a bad reputation. Employees can also feel uncomfortable and experience mental fatigue since they have to answer questions and complaints. The company must also spend a huge amount of money to regain its reputation, which surely reduces efficiency. The public might no longer trust a company exhibiting unethical behavior. History has shown that ignoring ethical behavior destroys a company much faster than when it develops and implements a wrong strategy but still adheres to ethical behavior.

Ethical behavior consists of corporate ethics, work ethics, and individual ethics. Corporate ethics address the relationship between a company and its larger environment. Work ethics address the relationship between a company and its employees. And individual ethics address the relationship among employees.

Ethical behavior will promote trust between a company and its stakeholder. This in turn enables a company to enhance its financial and non-financial performance in the long term. The existence of the company can also be maintained.

Paying serious attention to ethical behavior will create the impression that the company supports such a thing. Company policy is usually documented in a code of conduct. Today, as the world becomes more globalized and the demand for transparency is increasing, a code of conduct becomes more important.

Ethical behavior will thrive when there are agreements and understandings regarding behaviors that are considered right or wrong, as well as ways to help resolve ethical problems. There are three factors enabling ethical behavior to thrive in a company. First is a strong company culture. A company's culture is a set of values and norms guiding employees' actions. A company's culture significantly contributes to ethical behavior.

Second is the trust among the organization's members and between the company and its stakeholders. And third is the promotion of employee relationship management.

In promoting ethical behavior, internalization is needed. The internalization process consists of five steps: *awareness, understanding, assessment, acceptance*, and *implementation*. These five steps must be done in sequence.

A leader in a company must become a role model for the employees. If a leader pays special attention to the needs and interests of stakeholders in an effort to fulfill her responsibility to customers, suppliers, and other stakeholders, it will promote loyalty, honesty, and productivity.

There is a link between business activities and activities outside the workplace that influence not only employees, but friends, family, and society as well. Business decisions often have impact beyond work boundaries. Therefore, we can say that ethical behavior in doing business is part of not only corporate norms, but societal norms as well.

Promoting Corporate Social Responsibility

Corporate social responsibility (CSR) has been a topic of discussion over the last few decades. There are increasing demands from various stakeholders such as customers, employees, suppliers, communities, governments, and nongovernmental organizations. They expect companies not only to care about financial performance, but also to contribute to the well-being of society and the protection of the environment.

The European Commission defines CSR as "a concept whereby companies integrate social and environmental concerns in their business operations and in their interaction with their stakeholders on a voluntary basis." CSR is directed inside and outside of the company. Inside the company, CSR is directed to the shareholders and employees. To the shareholders, a company should strive to maximize shareholder value. A company should also address the well-being of its employees. Thanks to their hard work, dedication, and sacrifice, the company is able to perform many activities and succeed. Outside the company, CSR relates to the company's contribution in paying taxes, creating employment opportunities, improving the well-being and competence of society, and preserving the environment for future generations.

Andrew Tan in one interview with the *Philippine Daily Inquirer* on April 13, 2008, said that it was not enough to know your market and your customers. You must also gain the same mastery and understanding of your employees, suppliers, partners, associates, and even your banker and underwriter.

For companies, CSR brings various benefits. First, support from communities: Companies that carry out their social responsibilities consistently win the public's support. Should there be accusations of any wrongdoings, the public will most likely show their support. Second, CSR will help companies in minimizing the risk of any crises. Tsoutsoura (2004) suggests three kinds of risks related to CSR, namely corporate governance, environmental aspects, and social aspects. Companies that adopt the CSR principles are more transparent and have less risk of bribery and corruption. They will also implement stricter quality and environmental controls. Therefore, they run less risk of having to recall defective product lines and pay heavy fines for pollution. CSR also helps companies in reducing social risks. Third, employee engagement and pride: Employees will be proud of working for a reputable company that consistently helps societies in improving their quality of life. Employees will feel more motivated to work harder for the company's success. Socially responsible companies will also be able to attract and retain best talents more easily, reduce turnover rate, and lower the cost of recruiting new people. Fourth, CSR will strengthen the relationship between a company and its stakeholders, since it shows the stakeholders that the company cares about those things that contribute to its ability to operate and be successful. All of these benefits will in turn enhance the company reputation in the long term. This is despite the fact that CSR does not always have positive and direct impact on a company's financial performance.

The good news is that many Chinese family businesses are already aware of the importance of CSR. One example is IOI Corporation Berhad. Environmentally friendly practices are taken seriously by IOI Corporation. One example is its practice of returning empty fruit bunches and palm fronds to the land (Mason, 2011). This reduces the need for fertilizer by 40 to 50 percent and provides compost to enrich the soil naturally and to reduce erosion caused by rain. Another practice is the extensive use of kernel shells and fiber to provide renewable energy to produce the steam needed to extract the palm oil from the fruit. Nearly 98 percent of IOI's fuel consumption for steam generation at its mills is from these renewable resources.

Supporting and promoting education is an important area of IOI's CSR initiatives. These initiatives are mainly organized by Yayasan Tan Sri Dato' Lee Shin Cheng, a charitable foundation fully sponsored by the IOI Group of Companies, which was established in 1998. Through Yayasan Tan Sri Dato' Lee Shin Cheng, many social causes and initiatives are supported. IOI provides scholarships, gives out Young Achievers' Awards to outstanding and bright students to motivate them to excel in both academics and extracurricular activities, has a student adoption program that provides financial assistance to help underprivileged children, and sponsors schools under its School Adoption Programs.

Panda Restaurant Group is another example. In 1999, it established Panda Cares, a community involvement program. Since its inception, Panda Cares has given millions of dollars of in-kind donations to numerous nonprofit organizations, schools, and hospitals. Panda Cares' purpose is to promote the spirit of giving and establish a caring presence in communities where Panda Restaurant Group's guests and associates live and work.

Developing Estate Planning

Estate planning is the accumulation and disposition of an estate, typically to minimize taxes and maximize the transfer of wealth to the intended estate beneficiary. Estate planning is an important step to maximize one's wealth during one's lifetime. Estate planning must be well planned to anticipate unexpected events.

Since estate planning will involve many important decisions, not only ownership transfer but personal relationships as well, the best way to start the estate planning process is to determine the purposes for individuals, the family, and the business.

Estate planning has some purposes. First is to ensure that assets will generate income for those left behind. Second, to ensure that asset ownership will be transferred to the right parties. Third is to minimize taxes and other expenses. Fourth is to ensure that personal and family goals can be accomplished. Things that should be addressed in estate planning include equal treatment for all the heirs, ownership transfer of the business, tax minimization, and reduction of administration expenses. Change in life cycle should be considered as well.

For a family business, estate planning is an ideal way to maintain the continuation of the business after the owner is no longer with the company, as well as to maintain a harmonious relationship among family members. Estate planning should be addressed early because it will enable a family firm to identify which family members or outsiders have the potential to continue the business, to identify the training and development needs for the potential successor, and to develop plans for the transfer of power and management.

In estate planning, the first thing that must be done is to review the company's structure and ownership. As business grows and more family members are involved, organizational structure as well as clear job descriptions should be formalized. The role and authorities of the new owner or leader should be emphasized. Many transfers of ownership are often done without considering whether certain family members actively participate in the business or not. This could create dissatisfaction from active family members.

The next step in estate planning is to collect important data regarding the company. This includes examining personal wealth or capital used for business purposes, as is often found in many family businesses. Wealth that should be managed includes financial capital, human capital, intellectual capital, and social capital. Financial capital refers to the identification and understanding of responsibilities regarding wealth management, and also preserving family prosperity. Human capital refers to shared vision and values in the family. Intellectual capital refers to activities such as training and educating family members. And social capital refers to family values derived from society.

Next, prepare the financial statements, which include income statements, balance sheets, and cash flow statements, to check the financial position and condition. Asset liquidity to make transactions easier should also be addressed, as well as options to minimize the tax payment without breaking the law.

A common issue among heirs regarding estate planning is about profit sharing. How should profit be divided? To answer this question, there are some other issues that need to be clarified. Who will take over control of the company? Is he or she a qualified person? What if he or she gets divorced or dies?

In eastern society, which includes China, drafting written contracts or agreements to anticipate unwanted events such as death, incapacitation, and irreversible illness is still considered taboo or inappropriate. However, absence of such contracts and agreements often sparks conflict among family members, should any unwanted events occur.

In Chinese society, in which many still adhere to Confucian teachings, even though older brothers and younger brothers are not equal in their relationship, they all have an equal right to inherit the family property or assets. According to Yan and Sorenson (2006), one reason for this equal distribution is because the family requires that the entire family work together. All make contributions and all should be rewarded. Traditionally, it is assumed that daughters will marry and share their rewards with their husbands. Those inheriting family properties are expected to work together and cooperate.

However, we must recognize the fact that each family member doesn't make equal contributions. Some actively participate in the business; some do not. The needs of each family member related to his or her workload and responsibility should also be considered. Greater workload and greater responsibility require more money. Therefore, during estate planning is the time for Chinese family businesses to examine the contributions, needs, and responsibilities of each family member. The development of external factors should also be addressed since these will influence the business and individual wealth, directly or indirectly.

Chapter 12

The Future of Overseas Chinese Family Businesses: Toward a More Global Management Style

Globalization, rapid development of ICT, increasing competition, and the growing influence of Generation Y has brought tremendous change in almost all aspects of life, including in the field of business management. Today, there are more business opportunities as more and more countries open up their economy so that there are fewer barriers on trade and investments. Governments around the world are under more intense pressure to create a more favorable and business-friendly environment to enhance competitiveness.

Learning about business and management practices from successful companies around the world is easier since people can access more information faster than before. Today, many people are interested to learn about best practices from successful and reputable companies around the world, such as Apple, Google, Toyota, General Electric, and so on. These best practices are then often adopted according to the company's culture, field of business, environment, and resource availability.

Based on our consultation with some Chinese family businesses, we found out seven family business issues that they have often faced. These issues are value conflict, succession, organizational structure, compensation, competence, revenue distribution, and alignment between family and business. These family issues accompany seven common issues that are always faced by any corporation, regardless of size and ownership. The seven common issues are leadership; strategic planning; customer and market focus; measurement, analysis, and knowledge management; human resource focus; process management; and business results. The next generation will focus on the seven common issues and leave the seven family issues to the elder generation to work out.

The rapid development of technology has also influenced the stakeholders' point of view, lifestyle, and demand since they have become more well-informed. A company's stakeholders include customers, employees, the government, surrounding communities, nongovernmental organizations (NGOs), and so on. Each of these has its own interests that need to be carefully addressed. Nowadays, customers demand not only quality, but environmentally friendly products and services as well. Various surveys have shown that customers prefer buying products from companies that are socially responsible. Demand from the employees to be recognized and appreciated is increasing since they have dedicated their time and life to the company's growth and progress. Surrounding communities want companies to contribute more to the well-being of the society and to protect the environment. The influence of NGOs is also growing. They have become the outspoken critics of the company, particularly regarding the environment and well-being of the society. Not only have the stakeholders' point of view, lifestyle, and demands made companies more socially responsible, but they also have made them change their management practices, such as in marketing, production, human resources, and finance. This also forces companies to be more innovative.

Such situations are faced by companies all around the world, regardless of size, nature of product, and ownership. Overseas Chinese family businesses (OCFBs) are no exception. Moreover, most of them operate in countries or regions that have signed free trade agreements, such as Southeast Asia, Mainland China, North America (particularly Canada and the United States), and Australia. In order to survive and thrive, these family businesses must transform themselves; they have to abandon practices that hinder their development and progress.

Many OCFBs are adopting modern management practices, promoting professionalism, managing conflicts effectively, creating fair succession planning, and promoting ethical behavior and corporate social responsibility. Practices such as strategic planning, performance management, and risk management have become more common in Chinese family businesses. Today, such practices are requirements and expectations are set by the government, banks, and employees.

Although many OCFBs remain family owned and still reserve the strategic managerial positions for the family members, their management system has moved toward professionalism and modernization. For example, in addition to personal character, seniority, reliability, and trustworthiness, employees are evaluated based on their performance and contribution to business progress. Many OCFBs are also allowed more decentralized management systems, as suggested by Wijaya (2008). They also practice openness, including financial transparency. They are able to balance the company purpose of maximizing shareholder values and the family purpose of serving the family needs and interests. Many of them have already gone public. They no longer count only on family and friends of the family to obtain financial resources. In short, their management practices are sometimes not very different from western companies.

Traditionally, passing the business to the children was a means to make the family heritage last. But now, it is beginning to be seen as an opportunity for reorganization. Most of the younger generations entering the business are western-educated, are more critical about Chinese values and business practices, and are beginning to break away from the family network and conservatism.

As they do so, OCFBs are moving toward more universal management practices that combine the best of western management practices, where individuality is recognized, and fostering a Chinese family corporate culture where name and association are upheld at the highest standard. The question is, what about Chinese values? Does this mean the OCFBs must abandon deeply embedded values, such as Confucianism? The answer is: not necessarily. Some values will be maintained while others are adjusted to the right context. Values such as righteousness, commitment, filial piety, knowledge, integrity, honesty, working hard, bravery, modesty, and frugality should be maintained, indeed, since these have been proven to contribute positively to the success of the business. In fact, these values are passed down from the senior generations to the younger ones, although they are always described as Confucian values.

Familism is one of the values that must be adjusted to the right context. In Chinese tradition, familism has contributed to the strong family relationship, which becomes one of the strengths of a family business. Strong family relationships create trust, one of the elements in a healthy and successful organization. Familism also inspires family members to promote the creation of wealth, reputation, and glory for the family. As a result, family members would have a long-term orientation and avoid doing anything that may tarnish the family's good name. Familism also eliminates bureaucracy, makes decision making faster and more efficient, and creates more flexibility.

Strong family relationships and trust among family members should be directed toward efforts to achieve business as well as family goals. In other words, strong family relationships and trust should be the most important family and business assets. By ensuring this, the company can maximize the shareholder values, while at the same time serving the family's interests.

The future of OCFBs will very much depend on their ability to transform themselves toward modernization and professionalism, as well as maintaining positive values while adjusting certain values to the right context.

Currently, with the boom in the Chinese market, the global economy is dominated by the eastern countries, such as China, India, and Southeast Asian countries. Benchmarking is done both ways, from the western to the eastern. Many western companies are learning how to conduct business like the overseas Chinese, which shows their resilience during tough times, as well as their quickness to capitalize on the opportunities in good times, how to create a strong network, and how to instill values within their family. Many westerners are also curious about how the Chinese families build a close-knit relationship, are respectful to each other, and know how to help each other in the time of crisis.

Along with the growth of the Chinese economy and OCFBs, western businesses are now quick to learn about the Chinese culture. They are benchmarking the ways the Chinese are doing business and then integrating Chinese values into their business.

In the near future we will see globally intertwined management practices. The success of a company will depend on its ability to implement the best strategies and discard outdated ideas.

About the Authors

Dr. A.B. Susanto is the founder and a managing partner of The Jakarta Consulting Group (JCG). JCG is one of the most prominent local strategic management consulting firms in Indonesia, and has been around for over 30 years. He is also acting as a Commisionaire in GrowAsia Capital. Dr. Susanto is well-known for his ability to help big companies achieve their goals. His clients include some of the biggest players in their respective industries. Currently, he is an active board member in several organizations, both profit and nonprofit, and is the Dean of Economics for President University, Indonesia. He obtained his bachelor's degree and master's degree from the University of Indonesia and his doctorate from Duesseldorf University, Germany. He also received a PhD in Management from the University of Padjajaran.

Patricia Susanto is the current CEO of The Jakarta Consulting Group. She received her bachelor's degree from the University of Southern California in 1999 and continues her studies in Psychology and Human Resources at the University of Indonesia and Griffith University, Australia. For the past 10 years she has taken an active interest in family business studies and research. As a part of The Jakarta Consulting Group services she has worked on developing family governance for family businesses in Indonesia.

Bibliography

Allouche, Jose, Amann, Bruno, Jaussaud, Jacques, & Kurashina, Toshiki. "The Impact of Family Control on the Performance and Financial Characteristics of Family versus Nonfamily Businesses in Japan: A Matched-Pair Investigation." *Family Business Review*, 2008.

Astrachan, J. H., & Shanker, M. C. "Family Businesses' Contribution to the U.S. Economy: A Closer Look." *Family Business Review*, 2003.

Barclays Wealth and the Economist Intelligence Unit, Barclays Wealth Insights. "Family Business: In Safe Hands?" Volume 8, 2009.

Chan, Francis. "Family Businesses that Deliver." *Straits Times*, Friday, Jan. 23, 2009.

Cheng, Meng-Yu, & Lin, Yu-Ying. "The Effect of Gender Differences in Supervisors' Emotional Expression and Leadership Style on Leadership Effectiveness." *African Journal of Business Management*, 6(9), 2012, pp. 3234–3245.

Chen, Ming-Jer. *Inside Chinese Business: A Guide for Managers Worldwide*. Boston: Harvard Business Press, 2001.

Chua, Amy. *Battle Hymn of the Tiger Mother*. New York: Penguin Press HC, 2011.

Chua, Tony. *"YTL Land and Development Appoints Kemmy Tan Peck Mun as CEO."* *Singapore Business Review*, November 15, 2011.

Conley, James. "WIPO Case Study No. 3." *WIPO Worldwide Academy*, 2008.

Craig, Edward (Ed.). *Routledge Encyclopedia of Philosophy, vol. 7.* London and New York: Routledge, 1998.

Cruz, Jose Paolo Della. "Henry Sy Jr.: Beyond the Sy." *Philippines Star,* February 16, 2012.

Daft, R. *Organization Theory and Design.* Mason, OH: South Western, 2004.

Dyer, W. G. *Cultural Change in Family Firms: Understanding and Managing Business and Family Transitions.* San Francisco: Jossey-Bass, 1986.

Efferin, Sujoko, & Hopper, Trevor. "Management Control, Culture and Ethnicity in a Chinese Indonesian Company." *Accounting, Organization, and Society,* 32, 2007, pp. 223–262.

Ettorre, John. "Family First: A Company's Succession Plan." *Wells Fargo Conversations,* October 27, 2010.

European Commission. "A Renewed EU Strategy 2011–2014 for Corporate Social Responsibility." November 25, 2011. Online at www.ffi.org.

Flores, Wilson Lee. "Lance Gokongwei: There Can Only Be One Boss, and My Dad Is the Boss." *Philippines Star,* June 21, 2009.

Flores, Wilson Lee. *"Who Are the 25 Wealthiest Women in the Philippines?" Philippines Star,* November 6, 2011.

Fock, Siew Tong, & Wilkinson, Barry. "Over the Weberian Wall: Chinese Family Businesses in Singapore." *Copenhagen Journal of Asian Studies,* 25, 2007, pp. 99–125.

Gabriel, Anita. *"Groomed to Take the Family Business Forward." Straits Times,* January 23, 2012.

Gupta, Vipin, Graves, Chris, & Thomas, Jill. "Understanding the Internationalization of Family Businesses: Lessons from the History of Chinese and Lebanese Diaspora." *Academic Association of Historians in Australian and New Zealand Business Schools,* 2010.

Hofstede, G. *Cultures and Organizations.* London: McGraw-Hill, 1991.

Hyung-Jin, Kim. "No 'real' Chinatown in S. Korea: The Result of Xenophobic Attitudes," 2006. Online at http://english.hani.co.kr.

Hooi, Ng Si. "Malaysia's Richest Man Speaks Out." Star/Asia News Network, September 18, 2011.

Ikels, Charlotte. *Filial Piety: Practice and Discourse in Contemporary East Asia.* Stanford: Stanford University Press, 2004.

Jacobs, Jennifer. "1001 Commemorative Issue: Brave New World." *Edge Malaysia,* June 13, 2011.

Jennings, Lisa. "Having Words with Peggy Tsiang Cherng: Chief Executive and Co-chair, Panda Restaurant Group." www.findarticles.com, August 1, 2005.

Kaye, K., & McCarthy, C. "Healthy Disagreements." *Family Business*, 1996, pp. 71–72.

Knowledge@Wharton. "Many Family Firms Rely on Largely Invisible CEO—Chief Emotional Officer." June 27, 2007.

Lansberg, L. "The Succession Conspiracy." *Family Business Review*, 1(2), pp. 119–142.

Lee, Jean, & Li, Hong. *"Wealth Doesn't Last 3 Generations: How Family Businesses Can Maintain Prosperity."* Singapore: World Scientific Publishing, 2008.

Lee, J. "Culture and Management: A Study of Small Chinese Family Business in Singapore." *Journal of Small Business Management*, 34(3), 1996, pp. 63–67.

Lee, Jean. "Impact of Family Relationships on Attitudes for the Second Generation in Family Businesses." *Family Business Review*, 2006.

Limlingan, Victor. "The Overseas Chinese in ASEAN." Manila: Vita Development Corporation, 1986.

Martindale, N. "Leadership Styles: How to Handle the Different Personas." *Strategic Communication Management*, 15(8), 2011, pp. 32–35.

Mason, Cordelia. "Sustaining Competitive Advantage in the Oil Palm Industry: SWOT Analysis of IOI Corporation." *2nd International Conference on Business and Economic Research*, 2011.

McKeown, Adam. "Chinese Immigrants in Global Context." *Journal of Global History*, 5(1), 2010, pp. 95–124.

Mertens, Brian. "Forbes Asia's Businessman of the Year." *Forbes*, 2011.

Ng, Mary Kate. "The Man Who 'Flies Everyone.'" *China Daily on Asia Pacific*, May 20, 2011.

Ostrowski, Pierre, & Penner, Gwen. *It's All Chinese to Me: An Overview of Culture & Etiquette in China.* Clarendon, VT: Tuttle, 2009.

Poza, Ernesto. "Behind Every Great CEO: Shedding Light on a Spouse's Role in the Business." *Bloomberg Businessweek*, February 20, 2008.

Rahim, M. A. "A Measure of Styles of Handling Interpersonal Conflict." *Academy of Management Journal*, 26(2), 1983, pp. 268–376.

Rauch, James, & Trindale, Vitor. "Ethnic Chinese Networks in International Trade." *Review of Economics and Statistics*, 84(22), 2002, pp. 116–130.

Redding, Gordon. "Overseas Chinese Networks: Understanding the Enigma." *Long Range Planning*, 28(1), 1995, pp. 61–69.

Redding, Gordon. "Cultural Effect on the Marketing Process in South East Asia." *Journal of the Market Research Society*, 24(2), 1982, pp. 98–114.

Runes, Dagobert D. *Dictionary of Philosophy.* New York: Philosophical Library, 1983.

Schwab, Klaus. "The Global Competitiveness Report 2011–2012." Geneva: World Economic Forum, 2011.

Seymour, K. C. "Intergenerational Relationships in the Family Firm: The Effect of Leadership on Succession." *Family Business Review*, 6(3), 1993, pp. 263–281.

Shmavonian, Karl. "The Sky's the Limit for Teresita Sy-Coson." *Forbes Asia*, February 29, 2012.

Sidhu, B. K., & Kok, Cecilia. "From Dad to Son: Robin Set to Soar." *Star Online*, February 24, 2012.

Sorenson, Ritch. "Conflict Management Strategies Used by Successful Family Business." *Family Business Review*, 3(4), 1999, pp. 325–339.

Soriano, Enrique M. "The Chinese Way." *Sun.Star*, February 7, 2012.

Star Cruises. "*Star Cruises Chairman Tan Sri Lim Kok Thay Appointed as Honorary Professor of Xiamen University*." Press Release, January 10, 2008.

Studwell, Joe. *Asian Godfathers: Money and Power in Hong Kong and South East Asia*. London: Profile Books, 2007.

Sumardono, Andy, & Hanusz, Mark. *Family Business: A Case Study in Managing Nyonya Meneer: One of the Indonesia's Most Successful Traditional Medicine Companies*. Singapore, Jakarta: Equinox Publishing (Asia) Pte. Ltd. and PT. Bumitra Damardana, 2007.

Susanto, A. B., Wijanarko, Himawan, Susanto, Patricia, & Mertosono, Suwahjuhadi. *The Jakarta Consulting Group on Family Business*. Jakarta: Jakarta Consulting Group, 2008.

Susanto, A. B., Sujanto, F. X., Wijanarko, Himawan, Susanto, Patricia, Mertosono, Suwahjuhadi, and Ismangil Wagiono. *The Jakarta Consulting Group on Corporate Culture and Organization Culture*. Jakarta: Jakarta Consulting Group, 2008.

Thomas, Jill. "Internationalization of Australian Family Businesses: A Managerial Capabilities Perspective." *Family Business Review*, 2006.

Thomas, K. W., & Kilmann R. H. *Thomas-Kilman Conflict MODE Instrument*. Tuxedo, NY: Xicom, 1974.

Tsang, Eric. "Internationalizing the Family Firm: A Case Study of a Chinese Family Business." *Small Business Management*, 39(1), 2001, pp. 88–94.

Tsoutsoura, Margarita. "Corporate Social Responsibility and Financial Performance." Applied Financial Project, Berkeley: Haas School of Business, University of California at Berkeley, 2004.

Working Paper Series, Center for Responsible Business, U.C. Berkeley, 2004.

Vorabandhit, V. *36 Strategies of Dhanin Chearavanont*. Bangkok: Wannasarn, 2004.

Wah, Sheh Seow. "Chinese Cultural Values and Their Implication to Chinese Management." *Singapore Management Review*, 23(2), 2001, pp. 75–83.

Whitley, Richard. *Divergent Capitalism*. Oxford: Oxford University Press, 1999.

Widenbaum, Murray. "The Chinese Family Business Enterprise." *California Management Review*, 38(4), 1996, pp. 141–156.

Widenbaum, Murray. "The Bamboo Network: Asia's Family-Run Conglomerates." *Strategy + Business*, 10, 1998.

Wijaya, Yahya. "The Prospect of Familism in the Global Era: A Study on the Recent Development of the Ethnic Chinese Business, with Particular Attention to the Indonesian Context." *Journal of Business Ethics*, 79, 2008, pp. 311–317.

Woods, A. P. "Democratic Leadership: Drawing Distinctions with Distributed Leadership." *International Journal of Leadership in Education*, 7(1), 2010, pp. 3–36.

www.bukitkiara.com.

www.ffi.org.

www.pandacare.org.

www.toula.com.

www.sosro.com.

Yeung, Henry. *Chinese Capitalism in Global Era: Towards Hybrid Capitalism*. London: Routledge, 2004.

Yan, Jun, & Sorenson, Rich. "The Effect of Confucian Values on Succession in Family Business." *Family Business Review*, 19(3), 2006, pp. 235–250.

Index

203